ALBERTA REMINISCENCES

Marilyn-Valentine Brown

MINERVA PRESS
MONTREUX   LONDON   WASHINGTON

First Published 1997 by
MINERVA PRESS
195 Knightsbridge,
London SW7 1RE

2nd Impression 1998

Printed in Great Britain for Minerva Press

ALBERTA REMINISCENCES

This book is dedicated in twofold:

To my dear Mum, without whose help and encouragement I could not have continued when the book encountered 'rough passages' – she listened and said "No, that's not right, put this", or "No, do that", or "Yes, put that", "All right" and so on.

And,

To all my Alberta friends who have made my trips to Alberta so welcoming over the last ten years, and without whom this book could not have been written.

Contents

Author's Note

If I have caused offence to anyone in the course of the
preparation of my book – due to unavoidable errors in spelling
or any other unintentional causes (especially the Indian Nations),
please accept my apologies in advance.

Marilyn V Brown
11th November 1983
Coventry, England

Acknowledgements

Sincere thanks are extended to Miss Mary Loader of Winchester, England, United Kingdom, whose delightful design of the book cover has put the volume into perspective for me.

Grateful thanks are extended to the following companies and people for allowing me to use the Alberta Provincial Emblem and Tartan, names and photographs/drawings of places, properties, people and to those who pointed out my errors whilst compiling this book (which I appreciate very much).

CALGARY EXHIBITION AND STAMPEDE (John E Coulbourn, Publicity and Promotion Manager)
CALGARY TOWER (1975) LTD. (Paul A Pakos, Manager)
CHIEF OF PROTOCOL – EDMONTON, ALBERTA (John C Whalley)
CITY OF EDMONTON PARKS AND RECREATION (Ken K Kobylka, Director – Fort Edmonton Park)
DRUMHELLER AND DISTRICT MUSEUM SOCIETY (Ellen Manning, Curator)
HERITAGE PARK SOCIETY, CALGARY ALBERTA (R R Smith, General Manager – Heritage Park)
HRH PRINCE OF WALES (St James's Palace, London)
MINERVA PRESS PUBLISHERS
NORTHCOTT'S GUEST FARM, BALZAC, ALBERTA (Clara and Russell Northcott)
THE NAKODA INSTITUTE, MORLEY, ALBERTA (Fraser Pakes, Ethnology)

TRAVEL ALBERTA - EDMONTON, ALBERTA (Joanne Harvey)
TSÚ' TÍNA K'OSA (SARCEE CULTURAL EDUCATIONAL PROGRAM) (Harley Crowchild, Culture Director)
JOHN WRIGHT PHOTOGRAPHY (In Warwick, Warwickshire, UK, David Wright)

Maps and Sketches

N.B. All drawings, pictures, sketches and maps were prepared, designed, and drawn by author, except for the dust cover, and where indicated in the acknowledgements.

Lake Louise/Rocky Mountains/Alberta Rose

Introduction

I am a young English lady and have been very fortunate to travel at length over practically all of Canada, and especially Alberta – which is my favourite province – during the last ten years.

I recall one Albertan who was always taking me for 'a ride'[1] with the best of humour – on one occasion in July 1977 when my friend and I had not received our Stampede tickets, I made several enquiries about them. Whilst we were out one day, he took the following message for me, which will always remain in my memory with accompanying laughter:

---

[1] The term 'a ride' in English means being deceived.

"Calgary Executive Board telephoned to say the Stampede tickets were ready for collection on Opening Night, 8th July 1977 AD, accompanied by the 'Springer Express, Gone in the Wind'—"

Springer was, and still is, a favourite pony of mine and features in this book, although not called by name. I used to ride him cheerfully, despite all the mishaps which occurred when I rode him. He is a very old pony now and I have not ridden him for about two years, but I shall always remember him with affection – 'my Dartmoor Pony'.

The contents of this book are a few of my marvellous reminiscences during the course of my travels in Alberta, which I thought the Canadian people would like to share with me.

Foreword
I Have 'A Coat of Many Colours'

Akin to winter skies
After sunset has faded
Beyond the trees.

A new moon rises
'Like a sliver of glass'
In heavens, velvet black,
Dotted with hundreds of

Tiny shimmering stars
Amidst leafless branches
Of winter trees.
I walk across the yard

And gaze into the distant fields
Beyond the drive, and wait
For my heart to catch up with me
And the now, yellow half moon.

I have yet to see a
Full harvest moon, or even,
A spring moon,
Which would be nice.

A full winter moon is beautiful
As it rises higher and higher
Into the skies
Casting its light over the

Whole land of Alberta –
Across the silent prairies
And busy cities, and
Over me, standing quietly
Thinking of days gone past.

1882-1905
Creation and Foundation of Alberta Province

Alberta was created as a district in 1882 and founded as a province in 1905.

Province Alberta and Lake Louise were named in honour of Queen Victoria's daughter, Princess Louise Caroline Alberta, wife of The Marquis of Lorne, Duke of Argyll, Governor General of Canada in the late nineteenth century.

The Provincial Arms was assigned to Alberta in 1907 by Royal Warrant. The Alberta Flag bearing the official Provincial Arms was proclaimed on 1 June 1968 and can be used by any Canadian Citizen to the benefit of Alberta province.

Alberta's tartan was officially recognised on 30 March 1961 by the Alberta Government and constitutes green for the forests, brown for the rolling hills and prairies, gold for fields of wheat, blue for clear skies and lakes, pink for the wild rose, black for mineral resources of coal and petroleum.

Rosa Acicularis – Alberta Rose – was chosen in 1930 to be the Floral Emblem of Alberta. The roses grow in profusion all over the province in fields and road edges with varying shades of pink petals.

Alberta, Canada

(Sketch Map, not to scale)

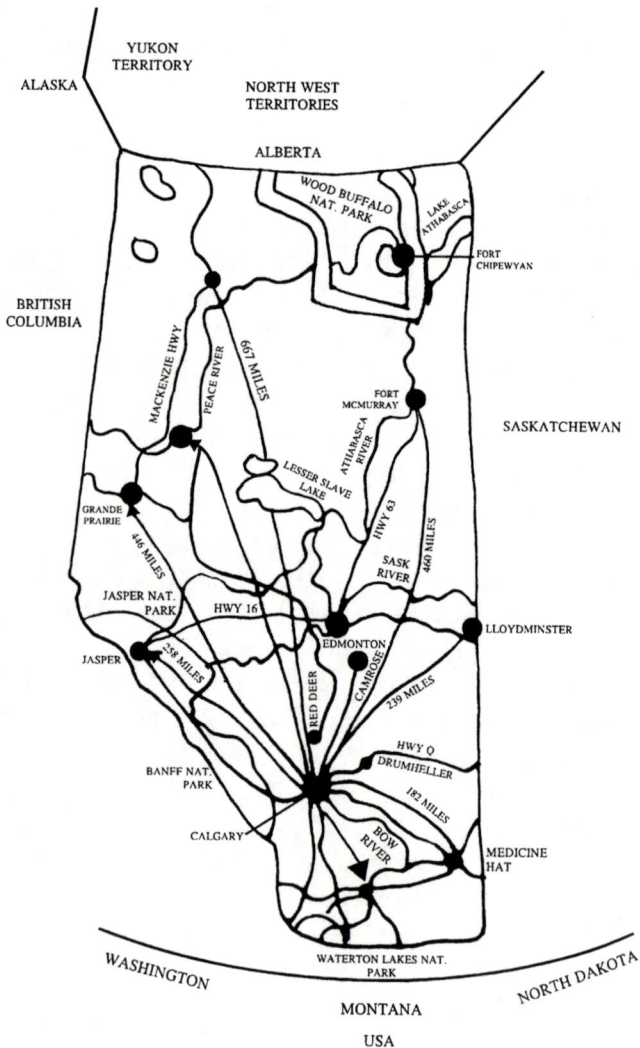

YUKON
TERRITORY

ALASKA

NORTH WEST
TERRITORIES

ALBERTA

WOOD BUFFALO
NAT. PARK

LAKE
ATHABASCA

FORT
CHIPEWYAN

BRITISH
COLUMBIA

MACKENZIE HWY

PEACE RIVER

667 MILES

FORT
MCMURRAY

SASKATCHEWAN

LESSER SLAVE
LAKE

ATHABASCA
RIVER

GRANDE
PRAIRIE

446 MILES

HWY 63

SASK
RIVER

460 MILES

JASPER NAT.
PARK

HWY 16

JASPER

258 MILES

EDMONTON

LLOYDMINSTER

RED DEER

CAMROSE

239 MILES

HWY Q

DRUMHELLER

BANFF NAT.
PARK

182 MILES

CALGARY

BOW
RIVER

MEDICINE
HAT

WASHINGTON

WATERTON LAKES NAT.
PARK

NORTH DAKOTA

MONTANA

USA

1972–1982

Introduction to the Land of Alberta

This covers many aspects of my nostalgic travels across the province of Alberta and is really an introduction to the many experiences I gained with various visits.

The Land of Alberta

Location: Mid-West Canada, surrounded by
  British Columbia to the west,
Saskatchewan to the east,
  North West Territories to the north, and
Idaho and Montana to the south

In ten years, I have covered many miles
Across the vast province of Alberta,
And, just cannot begin to mention
All the beautiful places I have seen.

I have become very much attached to this
Lovely province, and many people wonder why.
There is something there which
I cannot really explain.

Something continually calls me to return
To that province I love.
Alas, the ties of my home country
Are too strong to allow me to remain.

This land, to many,
Is flat and uninteresting,
But, to me, it is rolling, with
Vast plains of ranching countryside.

There are no trees growing, except
In foothills Forestry Reserves,
Or man planted trees on the ranches
Acting as a windbreak.

The skies are so vast and the clouds
In the west cannot be compared to
Other provinces, for there is something
In the formation which attracts me

Giving impressions of awe.
The storms during summer months are so
Spectacular, especially at night time,
Over the Rocky Mountains where the lightning
    forks.

There is often a cable or two
Brought down in a heavy storm,
And many places are without electricity
For hours at a time.

The violence of some storms
Really surprised me, for the
Hotter the land became in the day meant,
Generally, that a heavy storm was on the way.

Over the years, I have noticed
That storm violence has increased.
In the beginning, I used to enjoy
Sitting on a veranda

Watching as lightning played over the land,
Without rain this can become quite dangerous,
For lightning can strike anywhere
Without warning.

But, I now feel secure
Looking at the storm through the
Safety of windows inside the ranch,
Or homes of my friends.

Why, this last summer
We had a terrible storm
With terrific sheet lightning
So close, that we needed no lights.

The wind bent the trees almost double,
And many tiles came off the roofs
Of nearby houses.
We were indeed thankful when rains came.

Sometimes, there have been reports
Of tornadoes rushing across this land,
Now, that is unusual, I think.
I heard of one only this past summer,

Near Caroline.
The people saw it
Edge past the bottom of their property
And, had never seen anything quite like it before!

The beautiful snow-capped Rocky Mountains
Appeal to me very much,
The lakes, and waterfalls
Are numerous.

I was inspired by the beautiful
Waterton Lakes National Park
When I visited for the very first time
A few years ago.

I had chosen a busy day for my visit,
As many tourists dotted Cameron Lake and Falls,
Either boating or fishing,
Or, merely, just staring at the Falls.

The water was bitterly cold and crystal clear
Even though the sun was hot and
Shining brightly, very deceiving
For those who thought that the water would be
        warm!

I was fascinated by the reflections in the lakes
On bright sunny days,
Depending upon the position of the sun,
And have many lovely pictures etched in my
        memory.

All the lakes in Alberta have their own features,
And are just as beautiful
As each other.
Most of the lakes (but not all)

Have a small township
With tourist facilities nearby.
Lake Louise, in Banff National Park
Is one such place

With an attractive château close by.
Banff and Jasper have their own
Special features, surrounded by
The Rocky Mountains in all the

Glory of an alpine setting
Which persuades hundreds of tourists
To visit each year, both in
Summer and winter months, to enjoy

Both the splendour of the mountains,
And the added advantage of skiing
During winter, or cross-country snowshoeing.
There is an interesting Wax Museum at Banff,

Which gives the tourist an insight
Into Canadian history, and is worth a visit,
Or, maybe two, for the first time it is viewed,
The history does not remain in the brain.

There are the Banff Indian Days;
Hot mineral waters, open all year round,
The Sulphur Mountain gondola lift
Is certainly worth riding in,

If not for skiing,
Then certainly worthy of the magnificent
Panorama of scenery
Viewed from the lift.

Jasper, with its lakes,
Part of the Icefield Highway
And towering mountains of
Eisenhower, now called Castle Mountains

Are a joy to view,
Both on a summer's day
And a cold winter's day.
The Athabasca Glacier and

Columbia Ice Fields are an enjoyable
Pastime for the visitor, where
Snowmobile tours are readily available.
I remember with awe,

When I first saw these glaciers –
Never having seen a glacier before –
So white, and cold
Both in summer and winter.

There have been hundreds of
Tiny places in Alberta
That I have not mentioned visiting,
Places like Medicine Hat, Lethbridge and Airdrie,

But, if I were to write about them all
This would never be finished,
For each individual place has its own
Characteristics of great interest.

The city of Calgary
Is another great place
Which is located
In a bowl of the rolling hills

Where the climate is changeable,
Being governed by nearby Rocky Mountains.
Calgarians are very lucky
To live so near the mountains.

For all aspects of outdoor pursuits
Are readily available,
More so than in any other province;
There is hiking in the foothills,

Climbing in the Rocky Mountains;
Or camping by fast flowing rivers
And mountain streams;
Horse riding just about everywhere,

With everyone enjoying
Western style horse riding
And friendliness.
The Calgary Stampede and Edmonton Exhibition

Does much to promote tourism;
There are all sorts of local rodeos;
And Alberta Indian Days
Throughout the province during

The summer months,
Which are interesting to visit;
Fishing, cycling, canoeing, hiking,
So many things to do and see;

And, over the years,
I have attempted them all
And, can claim at being quite an expert
On the art of western horse riding

(Including falling off!)

The shopping too, is an exciting event,
I enjoyed the shopping in small townships
Where there are bargains in most of the shops
If you know where to look.

Jasper, to mention one such place,
Is a very pretty little town,
On the border of British Columbia
And Alberta, surrounded by mountains.

Oh! I could write many things
About Alberta,
But, I have mentioned only a few
Of the things I have found so enjoyable,

And, just look forward to my next visit
To renew old acquaintances, and
Hoping to make many more
New friendships in the future.

1972-1982
Introduction to the Alberta I Love

The inspiration for this came to me when I visited Alberta for one Fall and one winter season; the dawn and the setting sun has been a multitude of experience over the last ten years.

The Alberta I Love

My eyes saw
The rolling hills of Alberta
Which sweep horizons
Aglow with light from the setting sun,
Shared by the Rockies, sixty-five miles west.

A heartfelt sigh escapes me
As I breathe the scents of mother earth
All serene, on this lovely land,
Rapidly cooling from the
Heat of the day to the cold of the night.

I will never forget, on that cold winter's night
When I saw the beautiful orb of the moon,
Rising from the horizon, shining so bright,
And casting its light over me as I stood
Motionless on the sparse snows below.

The night was still, till a car sped by,
Breaking the silence.
A man with his dog, turned to stare at the noise
Breaking his reverie, as he walked silently by –
The car speedily vanished from sight

Enveloped by darkness.
Silence descended again,
An owl hooted in the distance, a coyote yipped,
Which re-echoed, bouncing off the hills.
The man and his dog continued, their breath

Freezing in droplets as it 'hit' the cold night air.
Majestically, the moon rose higher and higher
Into the skies, extending its golden light
Further over that huge land,
Covering prairies, the rolling hills,

And nearby Rocky mountains
Lightning scattered houses and ranches
Huddled at the base of the hills,
Their lights shimmering
In the darkness.

Temperatures fell, frost descended
Cold and cruel,
Damaging plants
Unknowingly left outside by an unwary rancher
Becoming blackened and shrivelled by dawn.

The night closed in, no animals astir,
I walked faster, coldness penetrating.
A sudden breeze
Rustling the dried leaves
Left over from Fall, startled me.

Shivering,
I drew in my coat
And ran to get warmth
Into my body.
My night's adventure

Was slowly turning to dawn
As the moon waned,
So the dawn approached
Fast from the east – picturesque in the early hours
The skies turning bluey-yellow.

A circled edge of golden sun peeped over the hills
Rising slowly, spreading its rays
Amidst the heavens
So blue and calm,
Reflecting the snows on distant mountains.

The air is cool, but the earth soon warms,
My hands were icy cold,
But I dare not stop
Till the sun was high in the sky,
And a bright golden ball of fire.

The morning dew was wet and cold
Upon my feet.
I hurried on,
Feeling I would be late.
At last!

I reached the clearing
Encircled by windbreak trees.
Our cabin stood, bathed in early morning sun,
A wisp of smoke curled from the chimney pot
Stealing into the still air.

Where have you been!
My Mother cries.
Exploring
Our vast land,
Said I.

(1875) 1972–1982
Introduction to the City of Calgary

Calgary began life as a humble fort in 1875 and when the population expanded to four thousand, became a city, or small township. When I first visited this city in 1972, the airport situated to the north of Calgary was small and the passenger area rather formal, with a corrugated iron roof.

I have many happy and sad memories of Calgary and watched the city develop over the last ten years with some feelings of regret, for somehow, the smaller city seemed more companionable than the large city it has now become.

However, I enjoyed my visits to the city, for despite its size, it has many advantages which I would never have experienced had I decided to stay away, including the hundreds of people I befriended on my shopping and sightseeing tours.

I felt I had to write about Calgary's colourful history, its present and the pride of its future heritage – and none of it would have been possible without the comradeship of my Calgarian friends.

The City of Calgary

Location: Southern Alberta near the Bow and Elbow Rivers

Part I

Her Beginning

CALGARY
Was 'born' in 1875
Beginning as a small Fort,
Named Brisebois after a

North-West Mounted Policeman
Established it
Near the Rivers of the
Bow and Elbow.

A Colonel Macleod
Commanded this Fort,
Re-naming it Calgary
After his ancestral home

On Island of Mull
Located in the Hebrides,
Scotland, British Isles –
Certainly a place to visit!

When the Canadian Pacific Railway
Reached Calgary,
It brought new migrants and
Pioneers who set up homes and schools.

In 1884 a township was formed,
With a Mayor named George Murdock.
Improvements in housing –
Tents and log cabins –

Was high priority.
Local sandstone was quarried
For the first building in 1887 –
The Knox Presbyterian Church.

Another famous place was
The Alberta Hotel
Located at 8th Avenue and
First Street South West,

Housing the longest bar in the West.
CALGARY CITY became established
When the population reached four thousand,
A Mr G E Orr was then elected as City
      Mayor.

The Volunteer Fire Brigade of 1885
Was replaced by
Professional fire fighters in 1908,
And, at that time,

The first electric streetcar
Began operating,
Serving some 35,000 citizens
Who were now living in Calgary city.

Law and order were the 'talk' of the land,
So, the North-West Mounted Police
Allowed the first police force to
Command in 1909.

With progression,
Modern police cars were introduced,
And the Royal Canadian Mounted Police
Were reserved,

Not only for ceremonial occasions,
But for policing of outlying areas too.
Trolley and diesel buses came into action.
Now, they are gone,

Replaced by buses, and, in 1981,
A new light rail transit system.
After World War II – in 1947 –
Calgary became a boom city

When oil discoveries were made
At Leduc,
Near Edmonton.
This attracted new residents

Which made Calgary city
Capital of the Canadian Oil Industry.
The Calgary Gas Flame –
Burning off of oil –

Used to burn in the Stampede Grounds,
But, for economic reasons
Was removed a few years ago, to
Turner Valley, south of Calgary and

The extraction of oil from Tar sands
Near Edmonton, remains the major
Oil developments in the
Province of Alberta.

Part II
Modern Twentieth Century Calgary

CALGARY – this modern city,
Full of tall skyscrapers
Nestling in a 'bowl'
At the foot of

Surrounding Alberta hills
Is a city,
Full of colour, history,
Hope and pride.

Twentieth century Calgary
Has much to offer.
A tourist attraction is the
Calgary Tower – known locally as

The Husky Tower –
Where visitors can shop for
Souvenirs, take refreshments
Or, an elevator to mysterious heights

To view the city below,
Both day and night
Through circular windows –
Seeing parks, busy roads,

Skyscraper buildings, the
Yonder rivers and countryside,
Especially the beautiful
Rocky Mountains, sixty-five miles west.

The revolving Husky Tower
Contains a restaurant which
Serves lunches and dinners.
Diners can see,

Comparatively easily,
The sights below
On ground level from
Different angles.

There is the Convention Centre
And museum, just across the street
From the tower.
The museum is a MUST for all to see

And portrays the life of a bygone era.
There are six floors filled with
Paintings, ancient and modern,
Eskimo carvings;

Indian tepees and tribal relics;
Pioneer life as it was.
On the first floor, a
Visitor can stand in awe

Gazing at the
Sculptured Aurora Borealis,
All in glass, reflecting the overhead light
And filtering sun from windows on high

Accompanied by that heavenly sound
Of high-pitched, gentle
Jingling –
The music of the planets.

On the outskirts of the city
The zoo is located,
With at least,
Twelve thousand species of

Different animals,
Living in spacious pens
Behind security fences,
Including the sculptured dinosaur.

There is a restaurant
Adjacent to the Botanical Gardens,
Where a visitor can sit awhile,
Enjoying the food and scenery,

The Planetarium
Was built in 1964,
And gives a good programme
For all to enjoy.

There are many parks
With beautiful gardens for
The visitors' pleasure.
The Devonian Gardens

Located in downtown Calgary
Are certainly worth a visit,
And can be visited from 8th Avenue Mall
Or from a nearby departmental store.

There are lots of beautiful flowers;
Tiny waterfalls, rockpools with miniature
Goldfish – many people throw in silver
Coloured cents for luck –

Seats to sit on, hidden in recesses,
Surrounded by tall green shrubs,
And manmade walls.
In winter, it is a hothouse,

But in summer it can become rather hot
Under the glass,
Even though a fine mist of water
Sprays over the plants,

And air conditioning is at its height.
Policemen patrol during the day
To see that the flowers and shrubs
Are not vandalised.

Shopping downtown
Is a great adventure.
There is so much to see,
So much to buy,

Many different things to eat,
Including wide varieties of candies
And different flavoured ice creams.
I found it hard to know what to buy!

Spring is slow to appear
And is welcomed by all.
The trees show forth
Their green mantles,

And the honeysuckle flowers open,
To the delight of the bees.
The lilac is gorgeous,
Its scent overpowering in the warm sun.

The weather in summer is sunny and dry
Although, there are occasions,
When it rains non-stop for
Days at a time.

The summer storms are awe inspiring
And sometimes, a nightly occasion,
With spectacular lightning, but
Storms are fierce and much damage is caused;

Power lines and telephones,
And even people,
Standing alone on the skyline,
Can be struck without warning.

The Fall is beautiful,
But as there are no trees,
Other than in gardens,
A visit to British Columbia

Or Ontario
Has to be made to
See the true
Fall colours of Canada.

The winters are hard and cruel
And, at times, the snowfall is heavy,
Lasting for days with temperatures
Reaching forty degrees below freezing.

December, January and February
Can be the coldest months
When cold north-easterly winds blow
And frost grips the land.

Calgary is lucky
Compared with other cities,
For she has the occasional
Chinook –

Bringing warm air and sunshine
Into the midst of cold winter days
Which is a welcome relief
To local inhabitants.

There is so much to do on a cold
Winter's night – a visit to the
Auditorium for a live show,
Ice hockey, or curling at the ice rink;

A night out with friends to see a movie,
Or, an evening at home with television.
The people of Calgary are fortunate,
In many respects to have such a lovely

Modern city which is fast growing,
Extending northwards and far south.
The Indians are becoming cultured as
Time passes, respecting western civilisation.

Calgary is a friendly city
Extending a helping hand to
Visitors from near and far,
Giving them the welcome they deserve.

And,
Hoping that one day,
These visitors
Will yet again, RETURN.

(1912) 1972–1977
Introduction to the Calgary Stampede

The Calgary Stampede commenced in 1912 as a small event and then became an annual event held every July.

I have a friend in south-east Calgary, now married with a family, and it was he who persuaded me to visit the Calgary Stampede should I ever come to Calgary.

The Stampede is an event I just felt I had to write about. It is so full of life, both from the pioneer spirits long past and the Calgarians of present day, striving to present their past history to the many tourists who visit the Stampede at its annual event.

Each time I visited the Stampede Grounds and watched the Parade downtown, I felt I had to portray my feelings on paper.

In fact, I am so GLAD I was able to come. I do wish I could visit the Stampede again.

The Calgary Stampede

Location: Stampede Park, south-east Calgary

The Stampede is an event
Which all must see,
And dates back to the year 1912
When an American named Guy Weadick

Suggested the Stampede
Became an annual occasion.
The Parade, then came down 8th Avenue –
And is normally held in July –

There are cowboys aplenty
Yahooing, up and down the streets
On their sturdy steeds,
And Indians from all tribes

In full war dress and paint,
On their horses and ponies,
Giving war whoops
As they ride bareback down the street.

At this time,
All the banks offices, stores,
And restaurants,
Are decorated

To revive the spirit
Of the Old West
Into the hearts
Of modern day pioneers.

The idea of this annual event
Is to remember
The ways of the pioneers
And how the West was run and won.

There are floats of immigrants
All doing their bit, and
The Royal Canadian Mounted Police
From the 'Musical Ride' follow, then

There is a brass band, or two,
With girls waving flags
Beating time with their feet,
Marching down the street;

And the man
On his Penny Farthing bike,
Old 'Klondike' Mike,
Followed by his mule,
Going slowly down the street.

There are horses and wagons,
Followed by the Old Beer Wagon
With a man on the front,
Driving the horses.

Pedestrians are waving
On both sides of the road,
Shouting encouragement
As everything goes.

The road cleaning machines
Are continually washing the streets
To protect those sitting on pavements
From dirt and dust as the animals walk by.

After the parade,
The crowds disperse
And go their separate ways.
Downtown, during the week,

There is a big 'line-up'
For pancake breakfasts,
And,
The noon hour Square Dances.

Colourful and full of rhythm,
With swirling skirts,
Checked shirts,
And blue jeans.

The violinist, piano accordionist,
And caller too,
"A dosi-do and promenade,"
"Swing your partners to the right!"

"Then to the left;
Link hands!"
"Form a circle!"
"Side step to the right!"

"Then to the left;
Girls leave outer circle!
Form an inner one,
Moving to the left!"

Whilst outer circle moves right,
Then reverse."
"Repeat it all again!"
And it goes back to the beginning once more.

In the mornings, afternoons, and evenings,
For the next nine or ten days,
The Calgary Stampede and Exhibition
Gets underway, having been opened by a
    celebrity.

There are chuckwagon races,
Bronc and bull riding,
Calf and steer roping, wild cow milking,
And track racing –

Sometimes, the
Royal Canadian Mounted Police
Have their 'Musical Ride',
Which is fascinating to see.

The events of the Stampede,
Are followed by a live outside show.
The days end with a magnificent display
Of fireworks at dusk.

Besides the Stampede activities,
The surrounding grounds,
Outside the arena
Portray –

An Indian village
With both adults,
And children
Living the life, of days gone by.

There is tanning of skins,
By smoking and stretching;
Working on beadframes for headbands,
Necklaces and insets on coats.

There are birch bark canoes,
And all kinds of traps,
Of course,
The bows and arrows are a standing attraction!

The women make the head dresses
With many coloured feathers,
Set into a beaded headband,
All ready to wear.

The men do the dancing,
And the beating of war drums,
The women do the chanting
Keeping in time with the beat.

The 'Chicken Dance' is a favourite with them,
So also, the war dance.
A circle is formed, and they move around,
In time with the 'music'.

For the war dance, wearing
Ceremonial dress, including war paint,
With tomahawks waving and drums beating,
They chant their war songs.

The war drums are beating louder,
The chanting also,
There are crowds of people
All agog at the show,

Thinking most fearfully,
Of those days long ago
When Indians tried to rule the land
By destruction of 'White Man's' property.

There is a lumber jacking area,
No real forest, just a mock display
Of men at work
On tall tree trunks.

A competition is held to find the
Best Lumberjack,
And the strong men of Canada
Fight with each other to take part –

And only the best man wins!

The other attractions
Are the champion livestock,
Both cattle and horses
Penned, but on show.

There are pigs, calves
And all sorts of things,
Including white rabbits
All munching away.

The Exhibition Halls
Are doing their bit
In beadwork, silver paper pictures,
And artists galore;

Selling their work,
Doing portraits whilst you wait.
There are leatherwork belts and
Cowboy boots of all sizes;

Stetson hats and others,
Lots of good food from afar,
Tempting the visitors from
Home and overseas.

There are cakes and candies
Old-fashioned and new.
Books and papers, pots and pans,
And sewing machines.

All displayed
On stands,
Just waiting –
For the unwary public to buy.

There is the Midway
(Local expression for
The Annual Western Fair)
Full of fun for all.

The cable car and Ferris wheel,
Far above the ground,
But not for those who fear,
To be at a great height!

Tickets for all rides,
Are bought from a central point,
Far easier
Than exchanging cash on the ride.

It is difficult
To remember,
All the rides there are,
For both young and old,

There is a lottery too,
For those, who wish
To gamble away,
Their savings;

Some are lucky, others are not.
A few go away with pockets bulging,
Whilst others,
Bemoan their lack of cash.

The Midway at night
Is a beautiful sight!
As soon as dusk falls,
All the lights come on;

There are reds and greens,
Yellows, oranges and blues,
Purple too, and white;
All moving throughout the night.

The visitor is sad
To leave the Stampede,
But a vow is made
To return.

Once the Stampede has finished,
There is nothing left
But litter – stub ends of lottery tickets
Even though, receptacles provided.

The stands are silent,
Animals and people have gone,
Wind rustles torn posters
Hanging from walls, all forlorn.

Another Stampede Year
Has come with all its fun
And has gone again
For yet another year.

(1914) 1972–1981
Introduction to Heritage Park (Pioneer Village)

The Park combines an authenticity of life in a prairie railroad
town and the lives of early trappers, miners and settlers seventy
years prior to 1914, but recreated in the mid-sixties for visitors.
I am very fond of the pioneering spirit in Alberta, and
sometimes wish I could have had the opportunity to step back
into history and be a part of it all.
My frequent visits to Heritage Park inspired me to write a little
of what I learnt and felt over the years, which I thought that
others would like to share.

The Pioneer Village

Location: south-west of Calgary

Heritage Park, colourful and historical,
Is situated south-west of Calgary
Jutting into Glenmore reservoir.
Portraying pioneer life in the 'Old West',
From the fur trading days
To the year of 1914 –
Outbreak of World War I.

The idea for Heritage Park
Dates back to 1961,
When trustees,
And officials,
Donated money and
Sixty acres of land,
For the development of the Park.

In 1963,
A society
Was formed.
This society was responsible
For the construction,
Operation, and development
Of the Park.

The society administers the Park
And is a non-profit organisation.
On 1 July, 1964,
The Park was opened,
For the very first time
To the public at large.

Heritage Park covers sixty acres
And, a hundred and sixty members of staff
Operate the village,
Each summer season,
As tourists
From all over the world
Descend on the complex.

There are over fifty restored,
And recreated buildings,
Vehicles, early farm machinery
Including all sorts of other equipment,
Furniture,
Artefacts and cooking implements
Which have been retrieved

From Alberta,
Other western provinces and
The north-western territories.

Indians, too,
Have their own special place.
There are tepees,
And lots of quaint
Old-fashioned things
Which Indians used to do,
For tourists to see and enjoy.

I love visiting Heritage Park
With its wooden entrance and
Flags of many nations,
Flying in the breeze.
There is so much to do!
You can see the women baking bread.
Then try a sample, or buy a loaf or two.

You can see the old-fashioned candy store,
Where I bought barley sugar twists,
Boiled sweets and humbugs;
I saw the hotel on the main street,
Where dinners are served in the dining room,
Or snacks in the bar,
And on the terrace.

Tourists can see
The schoolhouse, including old stoves
For winter heat, and furled
Canadian flags at the front of the classroom,
With blackboards and small desks arrayed,
Just waiting
For youth to fill the room.

The little church
Stands close by, and the
Operating blacksmith's shop
Where the blacksmith still shoes
Horses and does all sorts
Of welding jobs for the park,
And for anyone else prepared to pay.

A visit to the bank
Will offer you
An authentic certificate to
Commemorate your visit.
Letters can be mailed at the Post Office,
And will be hand cancelled
With the special hand stamp.

There is the water wheel,
And original oil tower,
Which explains how oil was
Found, and where.
A wagon ride
Is useful for the weary, and provides
Excellent means of transportation.

The old steam train
With its many coaches,
Takes the visitors
Around the perimeter of the Park,
And, occasionally,
Open parlour cars are included
For scenic viewing.

There are farms and ranches
Where visitors can obtain a good idea
Of how crops were grown – root crops too
Then stored, for winter use.
I found it useful to see how the
Herb gardens are sown, and also to watch
The herbs being dried and stored for winter days.

It is interesting to visit the
Early pioneer homes, and witness
The baking of cakes and cookies;
Jam making, fruit bottling;
Butter, cream and cheese making,
Using utensils
Of days long past.

I found it fascinating
Visiting the rooms where the
First settlers used to eat and sleep,
The patchwork quilts on the beds
Were beautifully made –
And I enjoyed talking to the ladies
Dressed in pioneer costumes,

Doing similar chores of those pioneers
Who used to live there so long ago.
There are many other wonderful things to see,
In this lovely setting,
Including a trip on the river,
Relaxing after a hard working day;
Shopping for souvenirs and Indian handicrafts,

Or, just sitting on a bench,
Enjoying an ice cream, or a cup of tea,
Maybe, just watching the people walk by;
All intent upon enjoying the life
Of a past era.

(1890s) 1972, 1977, 1981
Introduction To The Capital City Of Alberta – Edmonton

Edmonton, capital city of Province Alberta dates back to the goldrush days of the Klondike (1890s) which is celebrated each August.

Today's Edmonton is ultra modern, with the latest in design and technology, major commercial facilities and a light rail transit system, plus the 'Seat of Government' with its majestic Legislative Buildings.

I have a pen-friend in Edmonton, brother of a friend living in Ontario. When he married, he and his wife suggested I should visit them when I came to Edmonton – I never thought I would ever visit the city, but I did! So, the following events are of my experiences gained during my three visits to the city of Edmonton.

The Capital City Of Alberta

Location: Approximately 186 miles north of Calgary

Part I – Edmonton

I first viewed Edmonton one July day
From a bus on the main highway
High above the city.
We gradually descended from the heights
In zigzag fashion
Until we reached the bottom,
And found our way into the
Back entrance of the bus depot.

My first impression,
Some nine years ago,
Was one of awe.
It was a huge city,
With a small industrial airport
Right in the middle of downtown,
And, of course,
A larger international airport further south.

There are lots of interesting things
To see and do in this capital city.
So, where was I going to start?
At the library, of course!
I found out that Edmonton is Alberta's
Seat of government, and the home of
Canadian petroleum giants, besides clothing,
Coal, paper and pulp, including other manufacturers.

There was a lovely museum
Which I really must find time to visit
As it had a good history
Of the Indian nations
In the province of Alberta –
And I had always been intrigued by them –
There were Eskimo carvings and
Many good oil paintings of pioneer life.

My friends met me at the library and took me to see
Alberta's Legislative Buildings,
Built high on a hill.
Unfortunately, the hour was late,
So I could only view from the outside.
I saw a very stately building
Set in beautiful grounds,
Being floodlit at night,

Which showed up the borders of lovely flowers
And the province's emblem,
Laid out in flora,
Growing on a slope
For all to see.
Numerous other flower borders
Were attractively presented
At the bottom of the slope.

It almost seems like yesterday when
I paid my first visit to Edmonton.
Of course, it has changed a great deal in nine years,
And I was most disappointed to see in 1981 that
The Legislative Buildings, instead of being
In solitary state, were now crowded out
With other buildings nearby,
Thereby spoiling the effect

Of that beautiful setting
Which was held so long
By the Legislative Buildings.
We continued with our tour,
Visiting the University Campus,
Where my friend, until the year previously,
Had been studying.
This too, was a beautiful and spacious place.

In fact, I was reduced to envy
As the tour progressed.

Soon, we returned to their home
In Morinville, for the night.
In those far off days,
It was a quiet little place,
With no houses built at the back,
Just open fields and beautiful countryside,
Lots of wild flowers, insects
And wildlife.

But, now, nine years later,
This has all changed.
No longer can they see the wide open fields,
Instead, there is just another row of houses,
Packed tightly together
In a small township,
With several small streets
And many small stores.

The following day – 21st July –
I was taken to the huge museum
Which I had been looking forward
To visiting for a very long time.
I found that it was certainly worth
A visit and came up to my expectations.
We spent the whole day there,
Taking our time over the exhibits;

On 22nd July we paid a visit to
The Alberta Game Park,
Which was a huge place
With lots to see.
But, you had to be good at walking!
There were buffalo roaming free,
Rhinoceri taking a bath,
And a tiger romping through the trees.

I concluded my visit with a trip to the conservatory,
Located on the south side of the
North Saskatchewan River,
To see an amazing world of plants.
In the tropical house
We saw colourful hibiscus and orchids,
Palm trees, bananas growing –
A sight I had never seen before –

Gushing waterfalls, springs and little streams
Intermingle with flowers and undergrowth.
Fine mists of water continually
Wash over foliage and plants
In the humid areas
To maintain high humidity.
In the temperate clime –
Early Easter tulips and daffodils bloom,

With marigolds in June
And beautiful poinsettias in December;
Oak trees, horse chestnuts
And all manner of English trees grow here.
Following the slope of the paths,
We finally descended and stopped to look at
All the beautiful wildflowers
Massed in one huge carpet.

From there, we moved on to simulated
Dry desert country where tall cacti grew,
Rising high in the sky.
The only relief being,
In the flower of the cacti,
And the Burro Tail trees.
There are birds, too
Which flit in and out, in all of the zones.

At the entrance and departure areas
Of the conservatory
There are large containers, on stands,
Containing beautiful and most exotic orchids,
Which make you feel that you would like
To caress the velvety blooms.
There are containers of herbs, both with, and without
        flowers,
All named, for everyone to see.

Before I left Edmonton
I managed to visit The Planetarium
At Coronation Park; the City Hall;
And Elk Island National Park,
But I really did not get a chance
To see the big stores.
I have been back several times, but, somehow,
Never find time to shop: perhaps another day!

(1890) 1972

Introduction to Edmonton Klondike Days

Klondike Days date from the 1890s when men from Edmonton discovered gold along the Yukon Trail.
I never once dreamed that I would have the opportunity to take part in the Edmonton Klondike Days, it was sheer chance that I happened to be there when the events took place.
So, these are my feelings which I experienced when the events took place in 1972.

Part II
Edmonton Klondike Days

Klondike Days date back to the 1890s period
When gold was discovered,
By men who left Edmonton and went along the
Yukon Gold Trail.
Gold had been found earlier in 1860
When traces of it had been discovered in the West
Along the North Saskatchewan River
Bringing people from far and wide.

In 1962, a decision was made
To incorporate the Klondike Days
In the Edmonton Exhibition
As a tribute to past history
Of the province of Alberta.
I think the Klondike Days
Are a MUST on the itinerary of
Every visitor to Edmonton.

And I was very glad
I happened to visit Edmonton
At the time of the famous
Klondike Days in 1972
Where everyone dresses up
In the 1890's Klondike-style clothing,
Which can be either made, rented,
Or purchased at reasonable cost.

I recall, at this particular time
That at a certain period during the day,
Or was it the night?
If a tourist or local inhabitant,
Was not dressed in the appropriate
Klondike clothing, he, or she, could be sent to jail
By the sheriff, overnight,
Or fined a small amount of cash.

It was great to see
The marching bands
Of girls, all dressed in white tunics
With fur 'bearskins' on their heads,
White boots, each with a golden plume attached
At the front of their boots,
And carrying flags
In both gold and white.

Then there were the girls
Dressed in yellow straw hats and tunics
With thigh length green pleated skirts,
The first two carrying the Edmonton flag
And the third, holding the flag of Canada,
Followed by other girls
Playing the kettle drums,
And brass instruments;

There were floats of flowers
Covered with pretty dancing girls,
And the bath tub race
Oh! What a laugh!
The baths were of all sorts,
Different shapes and sizes,
Some on frames, and others
Just scraping along.

Sometimes there were two people in the tub
Or maybe, just one.
Each had a plunger
To help push the tub along
At a great speed.
At times, sparks could be seen
Emitting from the bottoms
As they rushed along;

The competitors
Were dressed in weird clothes,
Trying to keep their baths
On the straight and narrow path!
It all looked very difficult, to me,
To try and keep the bath tubs
All in straight lines
Going down the streets.

The pioneer-dressed crowds were in hysterics
As they witnessed the antics of competitors.
The general air of excitement was all around me,
As all sorts of people,
Tall, thin, fat, short and small,
Sunburnt and white all gathered around,
Cheering them on, in one great roar,
Which echoed across from corner to corner of the
    street.

I saw a stagecoach rushing downtown,
To collect money
From the bank.
It was exciting to see
The stagecoach in all its glory,
Clattering down the street
With shotgun lookout on the side, and pioneers
Seated inside, all enjoying the bumping jolting ride!

There was 'Klondike Kate'
Who came along and sang
Her heart out,
Accompanied by a fiddler,
Piano accordionist and banjo.
I posed with two girls,
One showing her garter,
And shrieked with delight

At the Can Can dancers
All dressed in brightly coloured costumes
Of yellow, and pink, with white plumes
On their heads
And each showing a garter encircled leg.
I visited, and joined in, the goings on
At Petticoat Pass,
Taking part in Square Dances,

And generally having fun.
We walked through Klondike Village,
Visiting old-time general stores and
Candy shops,
Then walked down the Klondike Boardwalk,
To the Klondike Palace Show;
Finally, ending up walking around
The exhibition grounds

Experiencing the fun of an old-time fair,
Watching the fireworks
At the end of the day,
But, our night had still not finished,
For we had the night-clubs to tour,
To see the gambling halls
In action, and
Singing the rest of the night away

With countless others,
Watching a cabaret show
Cramped high above the stage
In smoky atmosphere.

To me,
It only seems like yesterday
When all the amazing events of the
Klondike Days took place.
I have not been back again
As yet, to experience all the thrills
Of those marvellously exciting times,
Re-enacting the days of the past.

(1795 and 1802) 1972 and 1981
Introduction to the Fur Trading Days at Fort Edmonton

I had the good fortune to see the Seventh Fort Edmonton under reconstruction in 1972, whilst visiting friends in Edmonton. The Fort looked very different then from the completed Fort I visited in 1981.

I made my visit on a dull, overcast day in September 1981 with my mother and some friends from Edmonton. We took our time going through the Fort and surroundings.

The atmosphere of the Fort reminded me of the pioneer and American Indian days of the early nineteenth century and I felt compelled to write a few words of my own feelings at the time of this visit.

Part III

Location: South end of Quesnell Bridge at Edmonton

The Fur Trading Post

In 1795, the original Fort Edmonton was built
On the banks of the North Saskatchewan River.
It was a fur trading post,
And being built near the river was an
Enhancement to trade
Both by Indians and fur trappers.
Unfortunately, this fort was burnt to the ground
By Indians in 1802.

At least four forts were built
In those early days.
Fort Number Seven was being constructed by 1972,
Supposed to be opened to the public in 1973 –
I was fortunate enough to visit the reconstruction.
And, in 1981, I paid another visit to the Fort,
With my mother,
Seeing for ourselves

The excellent twentieth century construction
Made to look like a nineteenth century Fort.
We saw how the fur traders and their families lived
Inside the Fort;
Where the Indians traded their fur for supplies,
And smelt the hides being tanned,
Even seeing the fur press.
We had an opportunity to taste home-made bread

Baked in clay ovens.
I was fascinated with the way furniture was made,
And how the whole Fort was constructed,
For not one single metal nail was used,
Only handmade wooden nails
Bolted the furniture and Fort together.
The furniture was beautifully and
Lovingly made by good craftsmen.

Within the Fort there were three areas,
Lower, main and second floors,
And on most floors, a pinewood fire burned
In huge fireplaces, bringing an air of warmth
And happiness to the rooms.
With a bit of imagination,
I could almost see the original inhabitants
Eating food at the tables set for meals.

On all the floors, costumed volunteers
Made the Fort feel alive,
And we felt that we were actually part
Of that century long ago.
I loved my visit to the interior of the Fort
And wished I could have had the opportunity
To have lingered longer, or even taken part
As a costumed volunteer!

There were many things of interest
To see within the walls of the Fort:
The watchtower; the meat store; the chapel
(Which we found fascinating, as the lady there
Was very interesting to talk to
About the history of the chapel,
And wanted to know why we were so far from
     home);
The claybake oven; Bachelors Hall;

Ice house; married quarters;
Horse stable; boat-shed;
Blacksmith shop, his living quarters
And several other places.
We were beginning to feel quite tired
By the time we had visited all of these places,
And yet, there were still three
Historical streets to see, with boardwalk.

We visited three streets surrounding the Fort,
Some with the familiar boardwalk
Which I found so attractive.
All the shops, offices, saloons and so on
Had a distinctive air about them,
Selling all the old goods of a bygone era.
There were other things too,
A train   ride tour of the Park; a wagon ride;

Stagecoach tour, which we had to pay for,
But it was worth it,
To travel as they used to do
And get the feeling of being a part of it all.
Oh what fun we all had
On our tour of the Fort
Which has now been made
Into an extensive park.

I was really very sorry
When my visit to the Historic Fur Trading Post
Came to an end.
We had all enjoyed ourselves so much
And could really have done with having
At least a two day visit
Instead of an afternoon come evening visit.
A two day visitor's pass would be an excellent idea!

1972–1982
Introduction to Alberta's Four Seasons

I have been fortunate to visit Alberta in each season of the year, during the past ten years and felt I accumulated enough knowledge to write about Nature's signs according to these seasons.

I discovered that the seasons of late spring and early summer were the best, although Fall in all its glory comes a close second best, especially when the sun is high and the skies, that special bright blue, with everyone busy gathering in the harvest. Winter, too, held its special place in my heart as I traversed across the fields in search of the horses, but the epic tale of that comes later on in MY WINTER VISIT TO ALBERTA.

Seasons

Spring is the best time of the year.
The snows are melting slowly,
Lots of waterfalls and tiny springs mingle

With already formed falls and streams
In the foothills
With forests gradually greening with fresh leaves.

Slowly, the dark brown earth appears,
Followed by fresh shoots of green grass
Taking the place of the dead frosted growth

Which is all part of the winter months.
The undergrowth in the Rockies
Suddenly comes to life

And the layers of ice on
Footprints of last summer's hikers
Gradually melt away

Leaving crystal water and muddy ground.
Wild flowers appear;
Such as the 'Indian Paintbrush',

So prolific in this region;
Bog rosemary found in wet forestlands
Of Alberta; the small white mountain heather

On slender stalks,
And, in parts, a low dense, tangled growth
Of heather, comes to life rapidly.

The wild blueberry with pink or white flowers
Comes to life in June,
The fruit being enjoyed in August,

Or September.
There are many other flowers too, in
The lovely Rocky Mountain regions,

And other parts of Alberta
If you know where to look –
Even in parts of a cultivated garden!

A sudden Chinook
Will drive the remaining snows away.
The ground unthaws,

And the first crocus appears
Peeping above the ground,
Afraid that a late frost

Will nip their petals
Then, they will wither and die
And we will have to wait for another year.

Trees in the lower parts of the province
Have either died during the winter months,
Or, take on their fresh green mantle.

Daisies appear in the lawns,
Followed by the common dandelions
And the beautiful Alberta Rose

On short green prickled stem,
Growing, not only, in gardens,
But along the ditches and banks in clumps,

Or, on single, short, stems.
The sun slowly warms the cold land,
And farmers start sowing their remaining crops,

Praying for a good spring
To encourage growth,
And hoping for a warm summer

To yield a good harvest
In the far off Fall days.
The air is sweet with the perfume

Of earth's treasures,
Birds start building their nests
In the eaves of the houses,

And in a few man-planted trees
Scattered around in the gardens
Of cities and countryside.

Ducks and geese start flying in
From afar,
To build their new homes,

And stay awhile
On huge lakes
Away from the public eye,

Before returning to a warmer clime.
Calves and foals are born,
Jumping skittishly around;

Dogs start chasing bitches,
Puppies come into the world,
Baby bears, coyotes and wolves

All start new life
Free, in the wild
Of our great countryside.

Bees and butterflies
Come out of winter hiding,
Gophers and rabbits start

Scurrying around.
Mice come out to play
And are chased by farmyard cats and

Their kittens;
The odd skunk or two
Make their mark,

But do not live so long
If they come on farmland too often
Where the farmer has a gun.

All too soon,
Spring has turned to summer,
And the leaves on the trees

Have turned a darker green,
Becoming dust covered
From cars passing on the road.

The grass looks dry
And a stray match
Could easily start a fire,

Especially in the forestlands.
Fall enters the land
With a gusto –

August and September's
Harvested crops are safely
Gathered in and stored,

The rich, beautiful colours
Of Fall – red, rust brown,
Yellow and gold are

A delight for all to see.
Then, alas, the winter arrives
And another season is on its way.

1972–1982

Introduction to Signs of Nature Throughout Alberta Province

I encountered the following events at various times of the year near 'NORTHCOTTS' GUEST RANCH (as it was then called) at Balzac, five miles north of the city of Calgary and also at Sylvan Lake as well as the Rocky Mountains.

Part I
Alberta Rose

The Alberta Rose is one of the most
Beautiful and delicate of flowers
I have ever seen, being adopted by Alberta in 1930
To become the National Floral Emblem.

The roses grow in all sorts of shapes and sizes,
And all of them exuding sweet perfume
Made stronger by gentle showers of rain
Which fall on them throughout the summer
    months.

Roses have five large petals,
And a bright golden yellow middle.
The petals can either be pink or white.
The ones I kept seeing,

As I rode my horse through the tall grasses,
Were fresh and new,
Growing on short, prickly stems,
Scattered at intervals

Along banks and ditches,
Which, from a distance
Looked very attractive
Against the yellow grounds and green grasses.

Roses grow throughout Alberta,
Mostly north, but some south,
But the summers can become quite hot
In the south with no rains, and flowers die.

Seeing the roses growing so free,
Made me feel like dismounting from my steed,
To gather armfuls of these attractive flowers.

But, I consoled myself with just two or three,
Which I put in my flower press
For mounting in between plastic covers
When I returned home.

I saw some taller roses
Growing in bush-like form
At Sylvan Lake.
These too, were quite attractive

In pinks, reds and white
Towering above me,
As in vain, I tried to smell the perfume
Standing on tiptoe.

At the end of their season
The roses look sad,
As all their petals fall off
Leaving behind,

Faded yellow stamens,
And the beginnings of a large rosehip,
Yet, still green in appearance,
But, as Fall progresses

These hips turn from green
To a pale orangey-green,
Then to a pale red,
And, afterwards, a deep red.

The birds like to eat them,
But, we humans,
(Who know about such things),
Will gather the hips

After the first frost
(Or before, if they are ripe enough),
To make rosehip jelly or wine –
All good things for the winter store cupboards.

Soon, only the stem is left,
Which withers and dies
When the really cold, frosty, snowy weather
Advances onto the lands.

Part II
Clouds

How beautiful are the clouds
In Alberta's lovely prairies!
Sometimes they are so low
I could almost 'touch' them!

No other province has clouds
Quite like Alberta.
I can only describe them
As 'thunderheads', yet, they are not.

There are all kinds of clouds
Depicting different climates.
The Rockies, I am sure,
Play a great part in the weather.

The Chinook Arch
Means a spell of fine weather,
Which is typical of Calgary
And open prairie in Alberta.

Masses of clouds
Banking together, in rainy times,
Hovering low over the land,
Some of them are fleecy white.

The rest are usually grey,
Or bluish white,
Especially when the late afternoon sun
Shines upon them.

There is little cloud
On a fine, hot summer's day.
It can be sort of slanted
In lines across the sky.

Then there is the dull day
Where the clouds are white,
Turning to grey
And no blue sky to be seen.

There is the dust storm too,
Which comes up very fast.
One moment it could be a hot, dry day,
With cloudless sky

Then, the sun fades
As thick white clouds cover it,
A yellowish tinge
Invades the atmosphere

Turning the temperatures chill,
The acrid dust gets everywhere
Seeping through closed windows and doors
Covering the earth in billowing clouds.

Downtown the wind whistles
As it flies between the tall buildings
Taking all the garbage
And blowing it up into the air.

Fortunately, it does not last long
And skies clear rapidly,
The sun comes out, and
Clouds recede.

A snowy sky
Is easily detected.
It can be a brilliant hot day,
And, then, the next day, the

Sky can become covered
With thick white clouds
All taking on a
Yellowish hue,

And, before long,
The snow is coming down
Changing the hot weather
To cold, with the threat of winter days.

Sunset clouds can be varied,
Depending upon the heat of the day.
There is the stormy sunset
Where the skies are blue-black

With white cloud intermingling,
Slanting across the sky,
And the deep golden rays of the sun
Reflecting the stormy blue

And lighter parts of the sky.
The glowing rays cover the land,
Finally vanishing beyond
The horizon.

After a really hot, sunny day,
A sunset can become angry looking
If a storm is on the way.
The skies turn yellow,

Then orange,
Followed by a bright orange-red,
Fading,
As the sun finally vanishes from sight.

The visitor has seen nothing
In this vast land
Until he, or she, has seen the reactions
Of the mingling clouds

Not only upon the setting sun,
Or the dawn (which creates
A spectacular scene),
But, in everything.

Part III

The Skunk

A skunk is an attractive animal
Viewed from afar.
He is striped
Black and white,
With a long tail and sharp black eyes.

At least nine years ago,
Before housing from Calgary
Started expanding northwards
Destroying the peace of the countryside
And uprooting animal life,

There were a few skunks around.
They did not really do any damage
But, if they thought you were prey
You would do best
To rush away.

In those days,
I was young and innocent,
Thinking a skunk
Was just a pretty thing
Resembling a toy.

The two of us
Went out for a horse ride
One peaceful evening
When the sun had not set
And it was still warm.

My friend saw him first,
And could hardly speak.
She pointed her finger
And yelled,
'Get out of the way!'

'What for?
'It looks all right to me,'
Too late!
I found out why.
My horse reared and took a step backwards.

He was not quick enough.
Both he and I
Were sprayed
With a shower of fine stuff,
The smell of which was difficult to describe.

Except that it was so foul
It stuck up my nose for days!
'Phew! What a terrible smell!'
My friend cried,
Wheeling her horse away.

She galloped ahead, and left us behind,
To warn the others
Of what to expect.
Still unsuspecting,
I followed on behind,

The smell still with me
(And, I must admit,
It was pretty bad),
I arrived in the yard
Where a reception was waiting.

They made me strip
In the barn,
And I put my clothes
In an old bucket,
Full of Tomato Juice.

Then, I was marched upstairs
By my friend,
And, made to take
A bath of Tomato Juice!
Including, 'bathing' my hair.

Thank goodness, after that the smell went!
Now I am skunk-wary,
Although this year – 1982
A skunk passed by
And left his message, so strong,

At the side of the ranch,
Before I could close the window.
Ooh! It was awful
That smell,
Then, all the skunk memories came rushing back!

Fortunately, the rains came this night,
And washed the odour away.
The man of the house took his gun out next night
And shot the poor skunk
Which had caused the strong smell.

Part IV

The Coyote

I was walking past the bottom field this year
When I saw a flash of brown
In the dip
Amongst the growing crops.

I stopped, and stared
Wondering what it could be.
Yes, there it was again,
And, this time

Running at full speed.
It looked like a golden Labrador,
But surely not?
Or, maybe, it was a timber wolf?

A timber wolf?
No, far too close inland,
Especially,
When there were no trees

Or thick undergrowth
Where he could hide
From human beings.
Oh, no!

This looked like a coyote!
I could not believe it.
The last time
I saw one

Was at Big Hill Springs Park
In 1972.
There are several there
If you know where to look.

My companion told me
That, yes, it was a coyote.
They were timid animals,
But, for some reason,

This year, they had come
Quite close to habitation
To seek their food,
Being fond of small wild animals,

Or anything the humans
Left out,
Especially garbage.
They even looked on the garbage tip

To claw amongst the garbage
Which had been thrown there
By both people
And mechanical machines.

We watched and waited
Hoping for another glimpse
Of that coyote
So brave

As he wended his way through the crops
So thick,
Looking for that unwary gopher
Or a rabbit.

Alas!
It was not to be!
For that old coyote –
He loped off

Across the fields
Amidst the crops and grass,
Becoming lost from sight
Disappearing into the distance.

The land was still again,
With just the breeze
Stirring the heads of oats
And rippling the wheat and rye.

We continued our walk,
Gradually turning
Towards the ranch
And the hot meal awaiting us.

Part V
The Dragonfly

The dragonfly is a pretty thing
With two or four wings
Depending on size.

The one I saw,
Was one-and-a-half inches long
With a pair of wings coloured deep blue.

I was so close I could see the
Tiny, black, beady eyes
Which seemed to stare at me.

Sitting back on a pile of old fencing,
I watched it hover, then settle itself
On a blade of grass

In the midst of other tall grasses.
Its wings shimmered
In the sunlight, as it clung

By its legs to the blade.
At least ten minutes passed before it moved.
During this time,

I tried to capture it on film,
A still shot would have been nice,
But I could not get close enough,

As my shadow fell on to the grass
Where it lay
Frightening it away.

It flitted hither and thither,
Seeking a safe and sunny spot.
Unfortunately,

It eventually decided
To fly on its way,
And I did not see it again.

Part VI

The Dainty Blue Butterfly

I saw a tiny, pale blue butterfly
From where I was lying on the grass
Daydreaming, one late June afternoon.

It was a very pretty thing,
Which flew right over me
Landing in a nearby fir tree.

I waited and looked closely,
Hoping it would come nearer
To me, across the grass.

My patience was rewarded.
For it landed on the daisy patch near the barn.
I slid closer, along the grass,
Taking care my shadow did not fall on it,
And had a lovely view
Of such a beautiful insect,

Hovering off the ground,
Over the daisies.
All too soon, it flew off into the blue skies, out of
     sight.

Part VII
The Honey Bees

How I love to hear,
On a summer's day in June,
The drone of the bees,
Flying and settling on the honeysuckle trees!

It is amazing to see how the petals
Can carry their weight without falling off.
The honeysuckle trees
Were thick with flower this year.

There was white and pink,
None with perfume
Which the humans could detect,
But, thick with pollen for the bees' delight.

The many coloured lilac blossom in full flower
Has a gorgeous perfume
Which attracts the bees at a rapid rate.
We could smell the lilac at all times of the day

Including the depths of the night,
When all was still and quiet.
The night-time perfume of the florets
Could be quite overpowering

To the unaccustomed.
There were other flowers, and shrubs too.
The elderflower tree, and miniature apple,
Clover, white and pink are much enjoyed

By our friends, the bees.
Even the perfume of the nearby fir trees
Seemed to attract all manner of bees.
To me, the scent of the firs on

A hot summer's day
Will always remind me of my second home –
Canada.
The land of mountains and prairies.

Passing by a flower box
I noticed a strange thing.
Bees were piling into the earth
Where pollen must have dropped

From last year's flowers.
It was fascinating to see
These bees all on top of the soil,
Fighting for a place

Amidst hundreds of others,
Struggling to pick up the pollen.
As soon as their legs
Became coated with the pollen,

They flew off to their hives –
Both near and wide –
At the bottom of the garden,
Or, over the fields.

1972–1982

Introduction to those Lazy Days of Summer

This is really a collection of thoughts and feelings over the last ten years. I did experience the horse ride over the Alberta countryside, and I was often daydreaming of the good times now past, which I enjoyed, either on my own, or with a friend, or a guest staying at the ranch, besides myself.

So, it took little effort to write these few verses as I was 'seeing everything that I wrote' yet again.

Those Lazy Days of Summer

Location: In and around Balzac

The drifting, lazy days of summer
Are here again.
I gaze dreamily out of the window
Looking across the lovely
Prairie lands that hold endless dreams
Of the past –

"The air is so fresh and sweet
And the sun has yet to rise.
There is no hurry for an hour or two
So I linger on,
My thoughts far and wide.
I am riding through the

Long, lush, green grass
With a soft south-west wind
Blowing gently past my ears,
The sweet scent of the earth
Coming to me, and the
Butterfly, sweeping past,

Lying, pulsatingly,
On the fence post.
The trees are so green
In their first flush of youth,
As the dust of summer has yet to come.
The clover; vetch; wild pea; locoweed;

Cinquefoil; anemone and roses
Lie scattered here and there;
There is a croaking in the ditches
Filled with water at the roadsides,
And bubbles on the top
Signifying frogs living there.

Hovering high in the sky,
A lonely hawk
Looking for prey on
The wide lands below.
Coming to a halt at the cross-roads,
I rein in, and stop

To stare at the view.
We are high on a ridge
Which is exposed to winter gales,
The view is magnificent
Of rolling hills and fields
Filled with crops

Or lying fallow for a year or two.
Farms and grain elevators
Are scattered over prairies
Where once buffalo roamed.
I could see the golden ripening wheat
And brilliant yellows of other crops.

Ranches, like tiny dots
Lying in the valleys below,
Their windows reflecting the sun

'Like Indians flashing signals to each other.'
My horse is restless, but I want to linger,
Enjoying the view a little while longer.

In the valley below, I see a train
And distantly hear the fanfare as it
Crosses the road, followed by
A long trail of freight wagons,
Bound for far off places.
I breathe in the air, take one last look

Then, gently encourage my horse to walk on.
We walk down the road to that valley –
Which, alas, is no more,
As a brand new road has cut
Straight through, ruining the ridge
And all I remember –

Taking care to keep to the ditches,
As the road is busy with traffic.
Reaching the bottom of the valley
We 'cut off' across the fields
To find our own, special place,
Sheltered from wind, on the next hill –"

I come to with a start,
Realising that I am being called
To breakfast.
I rubbed my elbows
Where I had been leaning on
The open windowsill,

And stood up straight,
Remembering,
With a smile,
That I have many more summers
To look forward to,
Rather than dwell in the past.

1972, 1982
Introduction to a Summer Night Storm

The following events took place on my very first visit to Alberta, but the knowledge of summer storms in general are an accumulation of ten years experience.

I experienced this particular storm at the Guest Ranch (then about ten miles from Calgary), postal address being Balzac, where I first stayed, but have now stayed there each time I visited Alberta.

A Summer Night Storm

It is quite spectacular to see
An Albertan summer storm at night,
Especially near the Rockies,
Or in the foothills
Where it is quite severe.

I saw a spectacular storm
One summer night in July,
When I visited Alberta
For the very first time,
It was almost a welcoming committee!

This was quite frightening,
For I had never seen such a storm before.
The atmosphere was hot and still,
Not a blade of grass,
Nor branch of a tree moved.

It was about ten-thirty at night,
The sky was a deep, velvet black,
But no moon nor stars
Were shining,
And I had been sitting on

The wired-in veranda –
Wired to stop guests falling off –
Enjoying the peacefulness of the night
And viewing the distant city of Calgary
As forked lightning played around it.

To the west
Where the Rockies are located,
I could see sheet lightning
Lighting up the whole area.
Rumbles of thunder re-echoed around.

The storm turned in direction,
And started to come northwards
Towards us at a rapid rate.
The thunder became louder,
The lightning increased in severity;

And became sheeted and forked,
Not knowing which direction to travel in.
The whole sky was lit
With the colour of the storm.
A sudden breeze

Started to stir the trees,
Bringing a breath of coolness
Into the house
Which was, indeed,
A welcome relief

From the heat of the night.
Alas! The breeze quickly changed
To gale force winds,
And I could hear the hiss of
Lightning as it forked in the sky.

The storm's approach was so fast
That I was taken by surprise,
And hastily retreated
Inside
Shutting the double windows as I went.

Making sure that the bolts were
Firmly latched into position,
As the winds vented their full anger
On to them,
And, they visibly bent inwards.

I went into the dormitory
Which I shared with other lady guests
From all over Canada
And overseas –
We lived in with the family

And ate at their table.
I, and two other ladies,
Had actually retired to bed,
But as it was so hot,
I had gone onto the veranda for some relief.

However, it was obvious
There would be no sleep
For anyone this hot night.
I drew the curtains back,
And saw, hurricane winds

Bending the trees into horseshoe shapes
All across the yard.
It is a wonder that the trees
Did not break right off
And hurtle to the ground.

The thunder rolled incessantly
Around,
Receding into the distance,
And, then, cracking up
Right overhead.

We thought it would pass over,
But not so,
It just continued, on and on,
For hour after hour,
Without rain.

We had no electricity
As that had gone off
After that first heavy clap
Of thunder, and severe lightning
Striking the hydro[2] centre in the City.

---

[2] 'Hydro' is short for hydroelectricity.

They told us,
That, often, in a severe storm,
They were without electricity
For hour upon hour,
Becoming accustomed to it over the years.

The rain started to fall,
Gentle at first,
Then gathering force,
And pelting down
As hard as it could.

The noise upon the roof
And the rattling down the stove pipe
Was so loud,
That no spoken word could be heard.
We felt sure that we were quite safe.

Suddenly!
We heard water dripping.
Somewhere, something had sprung a leak.
I looked on my half of the room
And the others looked on theirs.

But, in the dark,
It is difficult to see.
However, we did possess
Candles and matches
Which were a great help.

We followed the noise
Down the stairs,
Discovering
All was panic
On the ground floor

A steady stream of water
Was dripping through the ceiling
From the dormitory floor
On to the table below.
Everyone was rushing around,

With buckets and cloths
Trying to stem the flow.
The man of the house
Tried to see where the water
Appeared from.

He said –
"We have a spring!"
But, his humorous words
Fell on deaf ears, as we were all so busy
Mopping up,

And a joke was no laughing matter.
I was very naughty,
As the situation struck me as funny,
And I laughed and laughed
Till I cried,

With tears streaming down my cheeks.
I tried to stop,
But it made it worse.
I developed a cough,
But just could not stop.

I fetched and carried,
Then made some tea,
Which we all shared on the job.
The rain stopped
Around three in the morning.

We all relaxed,
The carpets in the dormitory were sodden,
Bedclothes too, but it would have
To be left until daylight before the extent
Of the damage was known.

The yard was flooded
And mud merged into the grass,
Fortunately, we were
High enough off the ground,
So water did not come into the farmhouse.

It all seemed somewhat dead now,
At four in the morning.
So, with one accord,
We retired to bed, a good night's work done
Until the next bad storm!

1972

Introduction to a Ramble Through the Bow Valley Provincial Park

This was my very first weekend hike in Alberta – my idea of hiking and the Canadian idea of hiking are two different things. I found that the Canadians like to hike at great speed, whilst we English folk enjoy a more leisurely pace, viewing the countryside as it passes by. Not so, the Canadians, it seemed to me, they were always trying to race along.

However, despite the trials and tribulations I faced on this particular trip, the scenery was fantastic and I felt I had to recall my feelings at this particular time.

A Ramble through the Bow Valley

*Location: Bow Valley Provincial Park, approximately
north-west of Calgary*

A party of ramblers
From downtown Calgary
Left early one July morning in their cars
For a day hike
With a night's camp in the Bow Valley.

The climate in the Rocky Mountain regions
Is quite different from the ground level.
For there can be several climates
In the one day,
Such as snow at higher levels,

Rain and high winds
And such freezing cold weather
That thoughts of the deep frozen north
Would conjure a picture in the brain,
Of Eskimos and their igloos.

We left the cars parked in the lot
At the foot of the Rockies
And hiked up the hill,
With our faces turned into
The driving rain,

Which was icy cold, with quite big drops.
We huddled under a clump of trees,
Putting on our rainwear
Or heavy outer clothing,
Before we became too wet.

Turning up the collar of my coat,
I pushed my hands into my pockets
For warmth,
And waited with fourteen others,
For ninety minutes, hoping the rain would cease.

The rest of the party,
Eleven in all,
Returned to the cars
Unwilling to risk the cold wet rains,
And blustery winds.

The climate reminded me of England, somehow,
But I did not mind,
Although, many of the Canadians
Amongst our party,
Bitterly complained and threatened to turn back.

Finally, the rain stopped,
And we made our way slowly
Up the mountains
In the Bow Valley region,
All dripping wet.

Many of us became even wetter
As we brushed against the undergrowth
And were glad, to eventually
Reach a clearing,
Just as the sun broke through

From behind the clouds.
It was a pleasure to feel
The warmth of the sun
After all the cold and wet,
And soon, we became warmer and drier.

There were many pretty wildflowers around –
Gorgeous blue, pink and white daisies,
Indian Paintbrush flowers in bright red,
Lots of blue miniature lupins
And tiny roses.

We did a lot of
Fast hiking and climbing
Over rugged and beautifully scenic countryside
And I was enthralled
With the beautiful scenery I saw.

During the day,
I managed to have a 'good trip'
By falling over a concealed and
Moss covered log
With its roots outsprawled.

The rest of the party
Followed suit
As I was unable to tell them
In time
For disaster to be averted.

It caused some hilarity
Amidst a day of changeable temperatures
Both in climate
And in the feelings of
Our party members.

The day ended with a cook-out
On the banks of
The fast flowing River Sheep –
We were really very glad to relax
For an hour or two after our exertions of the
    past day.

Location of Sheep River, Bow Valley Provincial Park and Other Surrounds

(Sketch Map, not to scale)

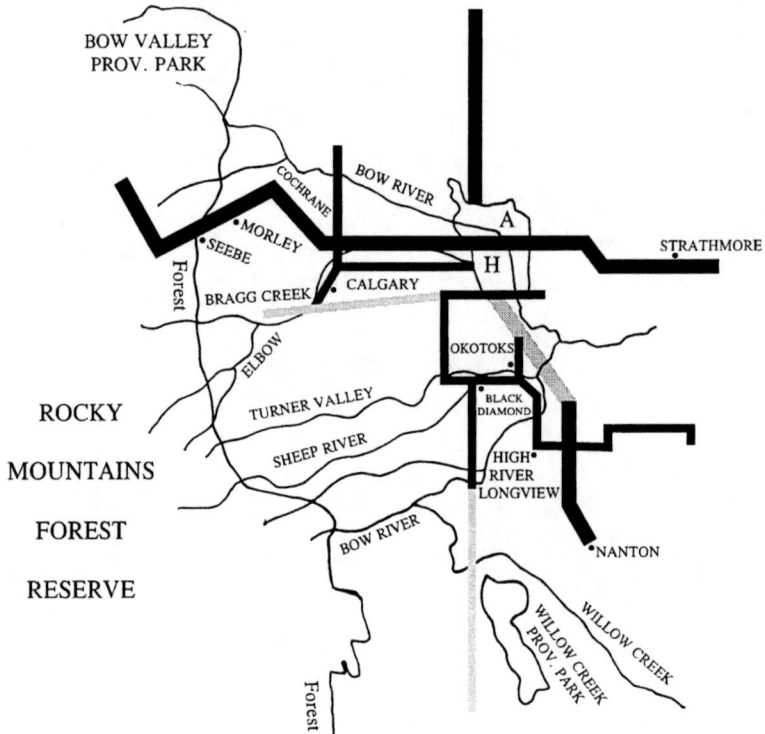

BOW VALLEY
PROV. PARK

COCHRANE

BOW RIVER

•MORLEY

•SEEBE

A

STRATHMORE

H

Forest

BRAGG CREEK   •CALGARY

ELBOW

OKOTOKS

ROCKY

TURNER VALLEY

•BLACK
DIAMOND

MOUNTAINS

SHEEP RIVER

HIGH•
RIVER
LONGVIEW

FOREST

BOW RIVER

•NANTON

RESERVE

WILLOW CREEK

WILLOW CREEK
PROV. PARK

Forest

KEY

PAVED ROADS	▬▬▬▬
IMPROVED ROADS	░░░░░
4 LANES UNDIVIDED	▓▓▓▓
DIVIDED HIGHWAY	▬▬▬▬
HOSPITAL	H
AIRPORT	A

1972

Introduction to a Night's Camp by the River Sheep

This was my first experience of a Canadian camp and things did not turn out as I expected. In England, we tended to take camp beds when we go camping, but here in Canada we just took our 'foamies' and bedded down on bare stone with sleeping bags and tents overhead.

I had never camped by rushing water before, so it was a completely new experience and the fear of bears too was a novelty (I never saw one at this stage).

So, I felt that I had to capture it on paper for all novice campers to read! Of course, there are a few details of a raw nature that I left out this time.

A Night's Camp by the River Sheep

We arrived during the late afternoon.
There were fourteen of us,
And we set up our camp
On the stony shores of the river bank.

The tents were erected in a circle,
With the flaps facing inwards.
We had no groundsheets
And our foam beds were directly placed on
      the stones.

We laid out our sleeping bags and gear
Stringing up a line between tent posts
For the coal oil lamp
Which would lighten our way in the dark.

The evening meal was prepared
And we each had our own special chore.
At dusk, we sat around the picnic tables
With the fir trees at our backs,

Laughing and chattering
We ate our way through a hearty meal,
Then washed up in the fast flowing river
Which rushed along at great speed

Stopping for no man, beast or bird.
The noise of the rushing water
Was continuous in our ears.
And, nearby, were the springs

Which gurgled and rattled
Over the stones
Finally, falling into the mighty
Rushing river below.

We hung up the leftover food
In an airtight container
High above the ground
So that the wild beasts,

Namely bears,
Would not be attracted to it
In dead of night
And disturb our slumbers,

For, although we were
Camped within the camp grounds,
It was quite bear ridden,
And, unless we followed all

Of the camp ground rules,
We could find ourselves
In quite a difficult situation!
As we had heard from some friends before.

We went in twos to the washrooms,
Which were especially fashioned
For the great outdoors
With no running water

Except for the river.
The toilets were twinned and quite dry
With just a perspex window
For filtering light in, through the roof.

Our ablutions finished,
We returned to camp
And drank hot coffee
By the warm camp fire;

Entertaining each other
With 'tall tales'
Which were enough to shrivel
The hair off our heads!

Then, feeling sleepy,
Two pals and myself
Retired to our tent
For the night.

I sank on to my bedcovers
Fully clad, adding more clothes
To my body for warmth.
Feeling utterly weary after my exciting day.

All night long
The sound of rushing water
Kept me awake,
No matter how hard

I tried to block my ears against
The sound, it penetrated.
So I gave up the idea of sleep
In the end, as it eluded me.

Instead, I lay there
And heard
The sounds of the night
Intermingling with the roar of the water.

We had been told
Not to leave the tent in the dark
On our own,
But to wait, if we could, until dawn;

I just could not resist
A peep out of the tent
Into the skies
To see a clear night

With stars twinkling,
And a large moon
Shining brightly,
Its shadows falling

On to the moving waters
And projecting rocks,
Making them glisten as the
Waters swept unceasingly over them.

I pulled in the flaps of the tent too,
Fastening them down,
And fell back on to my bedroll,
Awaiting for the dawn of a new morn.

1973

Big Hill Springs Park Adventure

I really needed no inspiration to write this particular piece at all. For this part of my trip over all the years I have been travelling in Canada, was most certainly the highlight of all the trips I have made – full of adventure and lots of fun.

Unfortunately, I have lost touch with the young lady with whom I spent a lot of my leisure time whilst at Balzac, so if she reads this, I do hope that she will recall the fun we had and write me a few lines, so that we can catch up on our past memories without feeling sad.

Location of Big Hill Springs Park, North of Calgary, Alberta

(Sketch Map, not to scale)

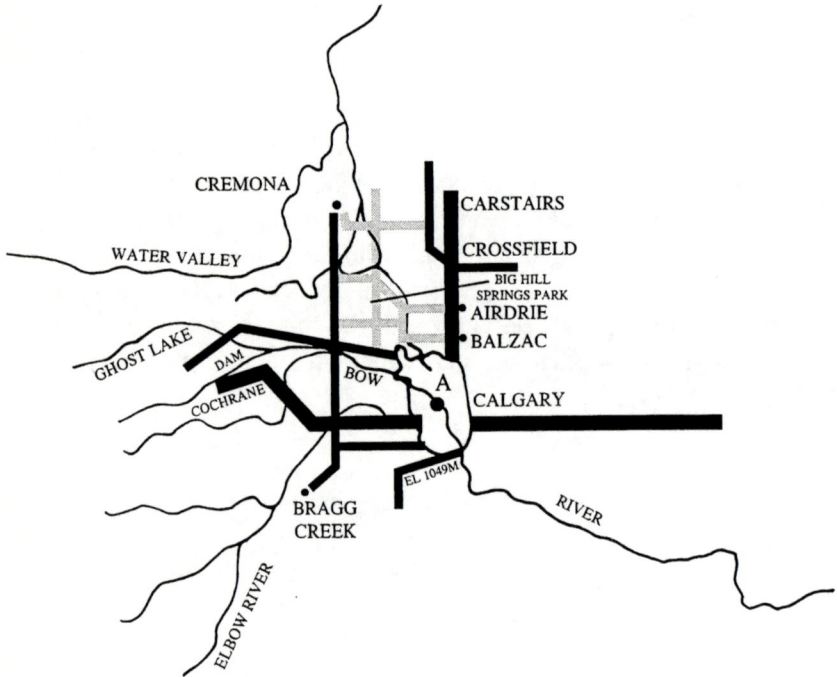

KEY

PAVED ROADS	
IMPROVED ROADS	
DIVIDED HIGHWAY	
AIRPORT	A

Part I
The Awakening

In late July and early August
My friend suggested
We take our horses,
Necessary equipment, and
Sufficient food
To embark on a long camping trip.

Neither of us had ever been
On this sort of trip before,
So we had to consult others
For advice upon how to organise the journey.
It took us three days to prepare
For the great adventure.

Our horses came first,
For they had to carry us many miles
Across rough country.
We made sure they were
Well rested, with plenty of
Food and water.

The day before we left, in the evening,
We went out into the fields
To catch the horses,
Leaving them well fed and watered
In the corral overnight,
For we would not have time

To chase after them in the early
Hours of daylight,
Not only would it wear us out
Before we had time to start, but
There would be too much noise
Disturbing the peaceful household.

We packed our bedrolls, blankets,
One large sleeping bag between us,
And polythene sheeting,
A can of water and a lariat each –
Like real cowboys –
For our food, we took

Two cans of tomato soup;
Spaghetti and cheese, beans, cherries,
Cheese; coffee; ham; bread; apples,
Oranges, candy and matches.
We took utensils, including mugs,
And food for our horses was a must.

At five past six next morning
We crept down the stairs
Leaving the house and
Taking all our equipment to the barn.
On the way out
We collected our blankets, bridles and saddles.

Eventually coaxing the horses with oats
To come to us,
We brushed, bridled and saddled them,

Then tethered the horses to the fence
Whilst we loaded our equipment.
How patiently they stood!

I suppose we should
Have had pack horses as well
To make life easier
For our sturdy steeds.
Mine was a black Dartmoor pony
(We suspected),

And my friend's horse,
Just brown in colour,
Quite docile,
Compared with mine!
And that was all we knew
About her horse.

It was a bitterly cold morning,
The skies were clear,
But there could have been
A slight frost, as the ground was
White in places and scrunched
Under our feet.

I was glad I thought to wear
My thick sweater and warm woollen gloves,
And thick woollen socks
In waterproofed boots.
I wore my Cowboy hat,
And my ears felt rather cold.

We climbed on to our saddles
And moved through the corral gate,
Closing it behind us.

Quietly we went down the gravelled drive,
Our tin cans, pots and pans
Jingling as we went.

Try as we might,
We could go no quieter
And fervently hoped,
Our going would be unnoticed
By the ranch inhabitants – we discovered later
That this was not so.

Part II
The Journey

We guided our horses south
At the end of the drive,
Heading for the forked road (today, everything
Has changed, and the road has gone).
Our progress was slow at first,
But we soon got underway.

By nine the sun had risen,
Becoming pleasantly warm by eleven.
Soon, we were shedding our warm clothes
And, feeling the heat!
We paused for a break,
Admiring beautiful scenery and wild flowers.

We saved our canned water
For such times as
When there was no habitation.
So, stopping a couple of times,
We asked for directions, and
Water at two ranches we passed on the way,

For ourselves and for our horses.
At one place we had a very cool reception –
My friend blamed me for
Stopping at this particular ranch.
Just because the ranch was well laid out,
Did not mean that the inhabitants were friendly!

I feel quite sure that the old lady
Who lived at the ranch where we stopped
And asked for water
Thought that we were going to rob her!
Instead of inviting us into the ranch,
As most Westerners do,

She took us down to the basement instead,
Giving us each a pail,
From which the horses drank!
We filled the pails with water
From a nearby tap.
It was well water,

Quite revolting, and musty in taste,
Compared with most well water
I have sampled in Alberta.
We wished we had not stopped for that final drink.
It might be all right for the horses,
But, certainly not for us!

We replaced the pails and returned the keys;
And without a backward glance,
Returned once more to our horses,
Clambering aboard with slight groans
For we were very stiff,
Despite all our exercise of the previous week.

We walked and trotted along the trail
Riding over pasture land,
Rather than open roads.

Our lariats came in useful for shutting
Barbed wire gates with a post at each end,
As together we could pull them shut.

After two hours we
Stopped for lunch.
Unsaddling and hobbling our horses,
We tethered them to a fence.
Then we found a shady nook,
Over the fence,

Against a bank of grass and trees.
We climbed over some barbed wire
Before preparing our lunch.
Alas!
I caught my blue jeans on the wire
And was left hanging upside down

In mid-air, unable to help myself
With threats of
'I will leave you there!'
From my friend.
Amidst gales of laughter,
She returned, to untangle me.

When we unpacked our lunch
I laughed aloud,
For the heat of the day
Had caused our cheese and ham sandwiches
To run into a solid mass,
And our cherries,

Which had been packed in a bag,
Had suddenly become pulp!
And the oranges

Were battered and completely unrecognisable.
Strange to say, the apples were untouched.
But, it did not matter, for we ate the lot.

We rested for an hour,
Then, brushed and resaddled our horses.
I found it hard
To resaddle my horse
With all the equipment still tied on –
Not so strong as I thought I was.

Part III
The Arrival and Settling in

We finally arrived at
Big Hill Springs Park about four in the afternoon
That same day.
I was stiff and tired
Being unaccustomed to long
Periods in the saddle.

Upon arrival,
We discovered
That horses were not allowed into the
Actual camping grounds
Of the park,
But, they could stay outside.

Before we made our decision of where to camp,
We galloped around outside
The restricted camping zone,
Up a steep hill amidst some trees
Looking for a suitable place to camp.
Finding an area

We proceeded to unpack and set up camp.
Well, everything was all right
Until we encountered the cows,
And found out we could not light a fire
To cook our supper on
Outside the camping grounds.

We had unpacked and hobbled the horses.
Unfortunately, one of them
Decided to slip his hobbles
And, promptly wandered off.
Whilst I ran after the horse,
My friend started to sort out our things.

Some cows with huge horns,
Wandered up to our gear,
And, above all things,
Started to eat my coat!
Stamping on our equipment at the same time.
We shouted and yelled, throwing small rocks.

Finally, we threw our saddles on the horses,
Bundling all our gear up into a heap
To get away as fast as we could.
I do not expect that the cows would
Have really hurt us,
For the local ranchers

Were allowed to loose their cattle
On the pastures green,
As long as they rounded them up
From time to time.
We led the horses downhill
As it was rather steep,

To the park enclosure.
It was at this moment
That I fell into a pitfall.

Instead of looking where my friend went
I stepped out across
A four foot wide muddy stream

My horse, being very stubborn,
Refused to follow
Despite all my tugs, enticements and threats.
I paused a moment to rest,
My back facing his head.
The cheeky animal

Pushed me hard with his head
And I fell,
Face downwards,
In the blackest, stickiest
And most slimiest mud
I had ever seen.

Coughing and spluttering,
I tried to push myself up,
But, I fell further into the slime,
Ruining my best gold bracelet watch,
For the mud,
Oozed well over my wrist.

Upon hearing the noise,
My friend looked up
And laughed, and laughed
Till she cried.
I threatened her with a handful of mud.
Eventually, I pulled myself out

Of the ground which
Had tried to claim me
With a sucking, squelching sound.
Sitting limply on the other side of the stream,
Covered from head to toe in black mud,
Completely exhausted,

Trailing the reins loosely in one hand,
Recovering my breath.
Then, that silly horse,
After all the tugging
I had done on the reins,
Moved forward at a rush,

Jumping over me! And
He set off down the hill
Without me!
I managed to roll on the grass,
Brushing off most of the muck
Sticking to my person just simply everywhere;

The mud did not smell too good,
And my white blouse was no more!
Hmm, so it was a good idea
To bring a change of clothes
After all,
And I ruefully surveyed the mess.

Much to my embarrassment,
The kindly ranger,
Having witnessed my struggles,
Had taken pity on us,
And chopped a large supply of wood
For our camp fires.

He did not 'do it for everyone', he said –
And had even been kind enough to
Lay the wood in the stone fireplace for us.
He enquired where we were going to sleep,
Not believing that we intended sleeping on the
    ground,
With saddles for our heads,

(Just like they did in the movies shown on
    television).
"What! No tent?"
"No!"
"But the dew is very heavy and the temperatures
Can drop so low. Are you sure you know
What you are doing?"

We assured him, we did,
And also, that we were very hardy.
"Yes, I dare say,"
"But, surely you are English?"
"Yes, but I am not so weak."
"Do not worry, we will be all right."

The ranger walked away
Shaking his head and muttering to himself.
Then, he returned -
"If you need any help in the night,
Come and give me a call,
And we will both come running."

I am quite sure if we had known
Just how cold it would become
During the night,
We would never have gone
On that trip
So unprepared.

We found a nearby picnic table, and benches,
And laid out our equipment.
Then we took care of the horses,
Making sure they were securely hobbled,
And could not take off in the night,
Even if they had a fright.

We were both looking forward to a
Hot cup of coffee and our supper;
So I pumped up the water
(Which was really a hard chore)
And we lit the fire after many
False starts;

Then put on the coffee pot to boil.
We stood two cans of spaghetti and cheese
On to the fire to cook.
Alas! We had forgotten our tin opener
Which we should have used
To bore holes in the tins

Before the contents were cooked!
I managed to force open the tins with
A selection of tools on my penknife.
Unfortunately, before I could bend,
I was showered with boiling hot tomato juice –
Which went beautifully with the black mud

As yet, still uncleaned, from my person.
Such as it was,
The food tasted good,
And we finished up with oranges
Which had become rather squashed;
The juice and pulp

Having seeped into our After Dinner Mints
Which fell to the ground as the bottom
Fell out of the bag.
There was orange pulp and mints adhering to paper
All over the grass –
But we ate them, paper, grass and all.

It was a long way to the water pump
Which was situated
Right at the other end of
The camp enclosure;
And it was even harder to pump up the
Water at great speed,

Which was necessary to get any water at all.
But it was worth the effort,
For the water was beautiful
And crystal clear –
Making it a most refreshing drink,
Much better than the musty water we had
  previously drunk.

Having drunk our fill and
Completed the washing up for the night,
We attended to our horses, then sorted out
Our beds for the night, deciding
To bank the fire up high to keep warm,
We hoped, all night.

Part IV
Night Sounds

We each had a large ground sheet and
Some polythene covering;
A blanket apiece; a sleeping bag
Between the two of us,
And saddles for our heads –
It is a wonder we did not freeze to death!

At nine in the evening we fetched more water to
    boil
Intending to try out an old American Indian recipe.
We had gathered some wild sage en route
To make some sage tea.
We had heard that it was an excellent brew
And would do us a lot of good!

Well, it may have worked with the Indians,
But it was certainly no good to us!
It was quite revolting
And we were nearly sick!
I think we used too much sage.
The brew was dark green in colour;

We put in eight lumps of sugar, but
It was still very bitter.
Not to be beaten, we
Had a mugful each
And drank half of the mixture,
Then tipped the rest away.

We had hoped it would warm us
All the night through,
But instead of that,
It must have been a stimulant
For we were wide awake for most of the night!
Hastily, we drank some water to drown

The awful taste
Wondering if we were on our death beds?!
Never again
Would we listen to those
Who told us
That sage tea was a good drink!

We put on all our warm sweaters,
Our woollen socks, gloves and hats,
Climbed into our makeshift beds
At dusk,
And tried, (my goodness, how we tried!)
To get some sleep.

Until you have experienced
Camping outside in the vast North,
The intense cold
Cannot be appreciated
By those, who spend all
Their days hugging a fire at home!

We discovered throughout the night
How cold and hard the ground was –
I declare the temperature
Went down to at least twenty degrees;
But the Ranger said the next day, that
It had only been thirty-five degrees!

We both lay there for an hour or two
Vainly trying to sleep.
It was a good job that we were camped
Close to each other, for the sights and
Sounds of the night
Were enough to give anyone a fright!

There were strange animal noises
Besides the lowing of nearby cows;
Green and yellow eyes
Flitted from place to place
(Unless, the sage tea had
Given us hallucinations!)

We heard the distant coyotes and timber wolves
Howling all around the hills,
One against the other, as if in competition.
They did not cease
Until the first streak of dawn
Cast its fingers across the skies.

There was no wind,
But we kept feeling
An icy blast,
And thought it was the spirits
Of the Red Indians
Long since dead,

But it was the polythene covering
Waving in the heat of the fire.
The fire became low as night wore on,
However, neither of us
Was brave enough to get up
And replenish it with wood.

So we stayed huddled together
For warmth during the rest of the night.
We saw several shooting stars,
And again, thought that
The Indians were shooting
Burning arrows at us.

We looked at the friendly rangers' cabin
With deep yellow lights at the
Uncurtained windows,
And wished with all our hearts
That we were camping on their floor
Instead of the hard, cold ground outside.

I tried so hard to sleep, but could not.
Glancing at my friend, I saw, that at last
She had fallen asleep, leaving me to brave
The sounds of night alone.
I gazed about me, and was delighted to see
A beautiful snowy white owl

Perched on the fence post a few feet away,
Its eyes, pinpoints of green, in the dark.
The rustlings of small animals were
Louder than usual as they looked for food,
Their eyes glowing yellow
In depths of night.

I heard the continual gurgling
Of the springs, and the shaking of the
Enclosure fence, as our horses moved
Up and down on their tethers.
My friend stirred and woke
After an hour or two,

"Oh! Is it morning yet?"
"Oh no, it is still dark!"
At each fresh sound we heard,
Be it some small animal
Or a sudden crash of sound,
We clutched each other.

"What is that?"
"Oh, it is only a mouse!"
No wonder we had no sleep!
Then, when we heard a growling sound,
That was almost the end.
We huddled together,

Shaking with fright,
Vowing to take up our beds and run
Into the night!
We never found exactly what
Made the noise to scare us so much, but,
Eventually, we fell asleep again.

It was an uneasy sleep.
However, I think I would have slept
All through the night
If my friend had not awakened me
With her gasp of
"Oh gosh!

"Just look at that!"
I thought there was a fire,
Or maybe, something worse,
But it was the most beautiful sight
I had ever seen in my life
And I was glad that my friend had awakened me.

Part V
Aurora Borealis

As long as I live
I will never forget
That wonderful night when I saw
The Aurora Borealis, or Northern Lights
As they are sometimes called.
This sight will remain with me

For the rest of my days.
No one had told us
That we could expect to see
Such a fantastic sight that night.
Of course, I had heard many times
About the Aurora Borealis,

But never did I expect to see it myself.
It all depends on the weather during the day.
This particular day had been very hot;
The night was clear and cold
With a star-filled sky;
And the great event

Took place about one in the morning
And lasted for an hour.
It is hard to describe
Exactly what it is like,
Except that it is
A luminous display of

Many different coloured streams
Of moving lights in the skies
All waving together
Sort of willowy, and gently;
So bright, that it
Lightens the land brilliantly

And the skies, too,
Where it takes place.
I do wish that I had put my camera
Nearer to my bed,
But I do not think that I could have
Operated the shutter

As my fingers were so cold.
It is the one and only time
That I regretted not photographing the event.
When it was all over,
We sighed long and deeply, getting up finally
To huddle over the fire with a mug of coffee each.

Part VI

The New Day

At four-thirty in the morning
When dawn had considerably advanced,
We removed ourselves from beside the fire
To go for a walk.
We walked in the park for about an hour,
Then watched the sun slowly rise

Over the hills,
Colouring the skies,
First orange, and then pink,
Finally yellow,
Then merging into the softly approaching
Blue of the new day's sky.

We found a cosy nook
Sheltered from the early morning cold air,
And fell asleep with our faces to the sun.
At seven we awakened, smelling the dew sodden
        ground,
And feeling the warmth of the sun
On our faces –

A welcome relief from the coldness
Of the night.
We were still warmly wrapped

Against the pervading cold,
Which would not disappear
Until the morning was well advanced.

On our return to camp
We saw a family of wild ducks flying
Towards the river flowing from the springs;
The sun's rays striking the water,
Casting reflective shadows on the
Dew covered ground.

We had hoped to have an early breakfast
But our return to camp was delayed,
By some wild bulls which had followed the
Cows down from the upper ridge,
And bulls were not to be 'crossed',
So we had to wait till they moved off the trail

Then made a dash for our camp.
The Park Ranger came round
To ask how we had enjoyed our night
Under the stars,
And to collect the fee for camping in the park.
He told us that it was the

Coldest night of the summer
So no wonder we suffered from the cold –
It was a wonder that
We did not freeze to death,
And congratulated ourselves
Upon our narrow escape.

We had breakfast
And put our bedclothes out to air
On the picnic benches; then we took care

Of our horses, returning to make up for lost sleep,
As the sun was now high in the sky and
Quite comfortable for our rest.

Awakening at eleven in the morning,
The silence was shattered by several cars
Arriving on the scene.
A motley collection of young children
And their teachers descended on the once
Peaceful green for their morning lessons in the open
    air.

We decided that it was time to exercise
Our horses for an hour or so
Around the park,
Fully aware of how
Inquisitive young children were
When it came to horses,

And, also, very aware
Of how our horses reacted
To small children!
Returning to camp a few hours later
We prepared our lunch of hot soup
When the temperature

Was about a hundred degrees!
We were supposed to vacate
Our campsite by one in the afternoon
As another charge would be made for our stay.
Fortunately, this was overlooked
By our now, kindly ranger friend.

We eventually left the camp grounds
At four-thirty in the cool of the evening.
As we made our way along the trail,
Clouds of dust formed behind us
And the rays of the sun
Were reflected in the dust.

Part VII
Homeward-Bound

It was a lovely uneventful ride homewards
Until darkness descended.
Then we had to take care
For the cars passed us at a terrible speed,
And we merged into the dark
Not thinking to wear something white

So that drivers could see we were there.
It became even colder as the night wore on,
And we could see
Electrical storms over the Rockies.
A splendid sight indeed.
Throughout the night we trotted

And did not stop,
Keeping to the main roads
Rather than cutting across country,
For in the dark
We could not see
The pitfalls, rocks, or, in fact,

Anything, that could easily
Cause our horses to fall.
We reached the perimeter of the ranch
Where we were staying
In the early hours
Of the following morning,

When, suddenly, my horse
Decided that he had had enough.
He reared, stamped, and pawed at the ground.
I did not dare get off
For fear he would run off without me.
It was at least half-an-hour

Before he calmed down sufficiently
For us to continue our journey.
Needless to say,
My friend collapsed in laughter,
But, I was not pleased.
We finally reached the warmth of the barn.

Unsaddling and unloading the horses,
We turned them into the corral
To fend for themselves.
And left all our gear
On the floor of the ranch,
Then, ate a huge breakfast and had a warm drink.

Before going up the stairs
We removed our boots and tried to make
As little noise as possible,
But, being accident prone,
I was my usual clumsy self,
And fell with a loud crash

On the stairs,
Which reverberated all around the ranch.
Everything I was carrying for a wash in

The bathroom, fell down the stairs,
One by one, till they reached the floor,
Then spun round once or twice

Before coming to a halt
With a resounding clatter.
It was all very well for my friend,
Who kept saying 'shh' to me for making a noise –
She just stood at the top of the stairs
In gales of silent laughter

Looking down at my plight
Without offering to help!
Even the dog came out of her basket
Wondering what all the noise was about!
I felt quite sure that the whole house
Must now be astir at the noise,

But no, no one stirred.
Truth to tell, they all heard, but
Being so tired, they just turned over in bed
And said,
"Oh! It is that girl again,"
And left it at that.

I finally retrieved
My bits and pieces, washed and so on,
Then, eventually retired
To my comfortable bed for a well earned rest.
Glancing across to the other bed,
I saw that my friend was already asleep.

I would certainly remember
Our adventurous horse riding trip!

1973

Introduction to Dust Storm

I shall always remember this particular experience as it is tinged with sadness, which made me feel that I had to write it down on paper.

My friend, with whom I went shopping on that particular day, was killed in a road traffic accident some months later, so I felt really thankful that I had taken the time and effort to meet her for our one and only outing.

Dust Storm

Location: Downtown Calgary and the outskirts of the city

I met a friend
And we caught the bus
To downtown Calgary,
Which is a very busy place
At certain times of the day.

We did our shopping
Then, suddenly the climate changed,
And it became very cold.
Being just in summer dresses
We felt chilled to the bone.

I am familiar with the climate
And always take a woollen sweater
Or jacket with me,
Which I hurriedly pulled on –
The climate is changeable owing to the Rockies.

The sky went grey,
Blotting out the sun.
It was so strange, and I wondered
What we were going to experience.
I soon found out!

A wind, gradual at first
Commenced, growing stronger
And fiercer by the minute,
Whistling between the tall buildings
Hurling garbage high into the sky.

Stinging dust and grit
Went into our eyes, mouth and nose.
We spluttered and rushed for shelter
Trying to get out of the cold blasts.
Everyone else had the same idea,

And all the stores were crowded out
With people seeking shelter.
Fortunately, the storm only
Lasted for half-an-hour,
The wind dying away as quickly as it came.

Everything reverted to normal swiftly
The dust settled and garbage lay on the ground.
Clouds cleared from the skies
And the sun came out,
Bringing a warmth to our chilled skins.

We heaved sighs of relief
And made our way to the bus depot
Homeward-bound.
On my return to the ranch,
I found chaos everywhere.

As it had been a lovely warm day,
All the windows were left open,
And the people of the ranch were out
When the dust storm blew up,
Consequently, a thin layer of grey dust

Lay all over the place
In every corner,
Over and under everything.
Even the bedclothes and curtains
Were full of grit.

We had a very hard job
Sweeping up the dust and
Shaking the grit from the bedclothes.
It was quite some time before we all became,
Or rather, felt, quite dust and grit free!

1973

Introduction to the Stubborn Pony

Being a rather accident-prone person, there are numerous incidents over the years which I experienced on my travels to Alberta that caused great amusement to my friends and their families. I have recounted a few of them amongst these pages as I thought readers would like to share them with me.

The Stubborn Pony

Location: The countryside around Balzac approximately five miles north of the Calgary city limits

It was not until I understood
The art of western horse riding
That I realised how stubborn
Some of these horses and ponies can be.

I took my small black pony
Out one day, for a short ride with my friend –
I preferred a pony
Rather than a horse

For the ground was not far away,
And, if I fell, I would not hurt myself
Unless I was travelling at speed –
We took our time down the hill

And came to a fast flowing stream
Which went under a bridge
Where we halted –
This bridge forms part of the road,

And the stream is no longer there,
Merely a trickle now
(Advancement of housing has spoilt
   this free land).
I waited for my friend to go first,

Which she did quite easily.
Then, it was my turn, but
My pony faltered
Right at the edge,

And I nearly became unseated.
I spurred him on,
But he refused to go.
I tried kind words,

And, then, I even dismounted
In an effort to lead him on.
All to no avail.
He just would not move.

So, what was I to do?
He obviously did not intend to stir.
I pondered,
Then remounted, kicking him very hard.

He started forward
At great pace,
Then stopped in mid-stream
With the water rushing over his legs.

He pawed the ground
And lowered his head,
Trying his hardest
To throw me off

Into the icy waters below.
I stayed my saddle
And coerced him onwards
With promises of an apple or two.

He moved one pace forwards,
Then, alas, his foot slipped on a rock
And, I fell
With an almighty splash

Into the water.
"Oh help!"
What was I to do?
I could not even swim!

My stubborn pony,
Unshackled at long last,
Took off
Leaving me there

In the middle of the stream,
Wet, miserable and cold.
He did not care,
For he was now 'home and dry'

On the other side.
I could almost see him laughing
As he bared his teeth as if to say
'I have done it at last!'

I hauled myself up
All dripping wet,
Feeling cold and depressed
As I squelched to the bank.

I looked at my pony
"You devil!"
I cried.
"You will pay for this!"

He let me catch him
And I mounted once more,
Much heavier than before,
Being weighed down with all the water

In my clothes.
I mumbled and grumbled
Under my breath
Vowing, that one day

I would get my own way
With him for a change.
My friend did not know
Whether to laugh or cry,

And, just as I remounted him,
He turned around and nipped me
On my most fleshy part.
Fortunately, his teeth did not grip

Sliding off
Over the tightly stretched fabric
Of my blue jeans.
However, I was left with a bruise

And imprint of a tooth!
To remind me of my stubborn pony
For the rest of my trip.
But what upset me most of all

Was the sound of
My girlfriend's laughter
Ringing in my ears as she galloped
Over the hill and out of sight!

1973

Introduction to an Evening Horse Ride

I can still remember this eventful horse ride as if it were still only yesterday when it happened!

The scenery, I recall, was so beautiful. In fact, I can almost smell the perfume of the crushed grasses and flowers as my horse's hooves galloped over them, and feel the wind rushing past my ears, blowing hair into my face and eyes, with my hat on its thong, halfway down my back, bumping up and down.

Then, that marvellous feeling of weightlessness as I flew through the air at top speed, before finally hitting the ground with a jolting thud, knocking the wind out of me.

Oh, no! I will never forget that occasion! Especially as I had to travel to British Columbia the following day covered in yellow, purple, green and black-blue bruises, aching from head to toe.

An Evening Horse Ride

Location: On the outskirts of the Balzac region,
which is north of Calgary

The four of us
Decided to go on a
Two hour horse back ride
After supper one evening,
As the weather was warm and dry.

There is nothing I like better
Than to ride
In the Albertan countryside
Where the air is so fresh and the
Perfume so sweet, from wayside flowers.

We saddled up our horses
In Western style,
Being all dressed in Western gear.
Mounting our horses, we clattered down the drive
To the road.

Crossing the road,
Into the ditch,
We went north, then turned west
Along the stony road
Until we reached another ditch.

In some respects,
It was safer to travel along a ditch,
But you had to keep your eyes wide open
For broken beer bottles,
And all sorts of garbage

Which people throw out of their cars,
For our horses were unshod,
And their feet, delicate.
Our horses were skittish
At the slightest sound,

Or, movement of waving grasses.
At times, each one of us
Had difficulty in controlling
Our horses,
For, they all had their own special ways

Requiring careful handling.
We walked our horses
In 'Indian file',
Along the bottom of the ditches
Being careful to be downwind

Of dust, from passing trucks,
Whose drivers yelled and waved to us
From their open windows,
As was the custom
When they sped past!

In the ditches, the grass was high,
Hiding potholes made by gophers,
Except, along the centre track,
Worn down by many feet.
And, the fields

With growing crops
Were shoulder high on either side.
Here and there,
Small flowers grew:
Wild pea, clover,

Both pink and white, and
The pretty deep, pink Alberta Rose,
Growing close to the ground,
On short stem,
All exuding sweet perfume.

Our leader decided on a gallop
As we reached the flat ground.
Off we started.
What fun!
To feel the wind rushing

Past your ears,
And smell the scents
Brought upwards
By the horses' hooves on the grass
And flowers.

Suddenly!
My horse stumbled,
And my reverie was destroyed,
As I was flying fast through the air
(What a lovely sensation, weightlessness!);

Coming to my senses
As I hit the hard,
Grass covered, stony ground.
I fell on my left side,
My head hitting a rock,

And my horse, just missing me,
As I rolled down the bank
To the barbed wire fence
At the bottom,
Stopping directly beneath the wire strands.

Cautiously stretching,
I found nothing broken.
Kneeling, before getting up,
I put out a hand
To catch the reins of my horse,

But missed, and he took off
As fast as he could.
I was alone,
Miles from anywhere,
With nothing but fields all around,

And, certainly no houses,
Or people, either.
What on earth was I to do?
I tried to stand, but could not.
For, my head reeled, my foot hurt,

So did my ribs.
I gave up, and lay on the bank
And waited.
Sooner or later, the rest of them
Would discover that I was not there,

And, hopefully, would return to look.
My horse did eventually catch up with them,
So they knew something was afoot,
And returned to look.
"How did it happen?"

Was their anxious query.
I regret to say, I was not
As observant as I should have been.
We were always told to look above
The horse's head between the ears, and

Directly on to the ground at the front
In order to spot danger.
Alas! I was going so fast,
I did not see the hole
All covered with grass.

Neither did my horse see or smell danger
Till the deed was done.
My friend told me
That I must get back on my horse.
"Cannot," I told her.

"You must!" said she.
"There is no other way to get back."
"Well, give me a while," said I,
"And I will ride again."
So my friend gave me a foothold

With her hands
And I clambered aboard,
Stiff, and all forlorn.
I was put on a leading rein to avoid trouble,
In case my horse bolted.

Then, we made our way
Slowly back
Across the lovely countryside
I admired so much,
Homeward-bound.

1974

Introduction to North Hill

Oh, the freedom I experienced galloping up that vast hill was marvellous. When you are young, you think nothing of doing mad things and you do not care what others think of you either! The excitement of those times seems to be so far away now that I hardly believe they ever happened.
I really needed no inspiration to write these forthcoming verses, it all came spontaneously to my finger tips, encouraged by the freedom of those happy hours I spent on the hill.

North Hill

Location: near Calgary

Nine years ago –
Although, it seems only yesterday
My friend and I
Used to horseback ride
On North Hill.

The month was July,
Usually warm and dry,
With a slight breeze
To ruffle our hair,
As we meandered up that hill.

The going was tough,
But we were fool enough,
To canter up there,
Coming to a stop
Long before we reached the top.

The grass was brown
On the top and sides of the hill
As there had been no rain,
But it had valleys
Of deep, lush green grass

Which our horses longed
To be released, to eat!
But we knew
We would lose out
If we let them have their way.

For their bellies would be too full,
To carry us on our way.
There were flowers growing
In the valleys of that hill –
Bramble and shaggy pink asters;

The wild purple lupin
And Alberta Rose
Lying close to the ground,
Its pink petals and yellow centres
So attractive against the green grass.

No trees grew here,
So, no shade.
It was wide open to all the four winds,
But, at the time we were there,
It was hot at noon day.

We dismounted,
Leading the horses downhill
Till we found a suitable spot
To unsaddle
And let the horses cool off.

We gave them a quick drink
Of water from our hats,
And unpacked our lunch,
Eating in silence,
Admiring the view

Of distant Calgary
Shrouded in heat mist.
We rested an hour,
Then, slowly turned,
To go back

Down that 'Old Hill'.
The horses were reluctant
To accept the saddles again
Preferring to be free,
To roll on the hill.

Clouds suddenly formed,
The air grew still,
And the sky became black.
A distant rumble of thunder
Soon had us galloping downwards.

For it was no joke to be caught in a storm
On wide open spaces.
We reached the flat land
Just in time, the hill behind us
And the rain surrounded us.

Alas, today,
We can ride no more,
For houses are now being built on the hill.
The power lines too,
Are making their mark,

And a new road has become
Established at the foot of the hill
Making access impossible
At all times of the day
For horses and riders.

I feel sad, somehow,
For part of my life
Has gone for ever.
Never again will I have the chance
To horse ride madly up North Hill.

1974

Introduction to the Garbage Dump

Part of the following is true and the rest of it is fiction. Lots of people used to get out to this particular garbage dump to practise shooting, both at actual targets and ones they set up themselves. At one stage, it really became quite dangerous for anyone to even be allowed to dump their garbage.

My friend and I used to do lots of horse riding here, because we thought it was an exciting place to ride in as long as we took care to avoid the rifle shots flying around us.

The latter half of my write-up on this section is fictitious because I do not suppose for one moment that either my friend or myself would ever be able to lasso a fellow with a rope let alone drag him along behind a horse!

The Garbage Dump

Location: just outside Calgary

My friend and I
Used to horseback ride
At a forbidden place
A few years ago.
This was exciting to us,

For, besides being a dump,
There were hidden valleys,
Huge rocks to negotiate
And a wild coyote or two
Running about, here and there.

We imagined we were fleeing
From the sheriff and his men,
As shots whizzed past
From above,
To strike the rocks with a twang!

We moved faster
To get out of the way,
Only to find,
Our entrance blocked
By a garbage dumper.

201

"What are you two
Doing here?"
The man cried.
"Did you not see the sign?"
"No," we replied, uncomfortably.

It had been torn down,
But the stump was still there.
We twisted in our saddles,
Anxious to get away and hide.
The bullets had stopped,

But we were still afraid,
As the man told us,
To go back the way we came.
We explained our fears.
It was no good, for he did not listen.

Back we went, keeping a keen eye open
For marauding strangers.
Crack! went a gun.
Twang! went the bullet,
Just missing my arm by an inch.

"Hurry! Let us get out of here!"
My friend cried.
"How can we?" I replied,
"For we are in a bad position
Down in the valley, with the rocks above."

"Perhaps we can skirt the perimeter
Of the valley
And cut them off from behind."
Said my cheerful friend,
Never seeing danger until we were doomed!

So we wheeled our horses
Through thicket and scrub trees,
We did our best and
Eventually came out on the top,
Behind the boys who had scared us.

We thought for a minute,
Then unravelled our lariats
Which we always took with us
In case of an emergency,
And spun them

In a silent circle.
My friend went for one boy,
And I went for the other.
They did not suspect
So we caught them, both on target!

They dropped their rifles
In great surprise,
Amazed that we had surprised them.
"Do you want to come quietly,
Or shall we truss you like the Indians did

And drag you behind our horses,
To the dumper at the entrance?"
There was no sound, as they thought
Of their plight,
For they knew they were as much at fault as we.

"We promise to go quietly,
If you will let us go."
We agreed, but on one condition,
"If you want to use your rifles,
Come out to the ranch where it is safer."

They agreed quite willingly.
So we let them go
And continued on our way,
Still enjoying the valleys
Where the wild things grew.

It is sad, over the years
How things change,
Where once there was freedom,
Now, there are restrictions,
And, no longer can we ride over the dump.

We had such fun in those
Few short years
With our horses
And our friends,
But now, houses have been built on the dump,

And the valleys have been landscaped
Becoming part of peoples' gardens.
The dump is no more –
It has moved to another site
Where security is tight.

Location of Drumheller Valley in the Red Deer River Valley of Eastern Alberta – Known as 'The Badlands'

(Sketch Map, not to scale)

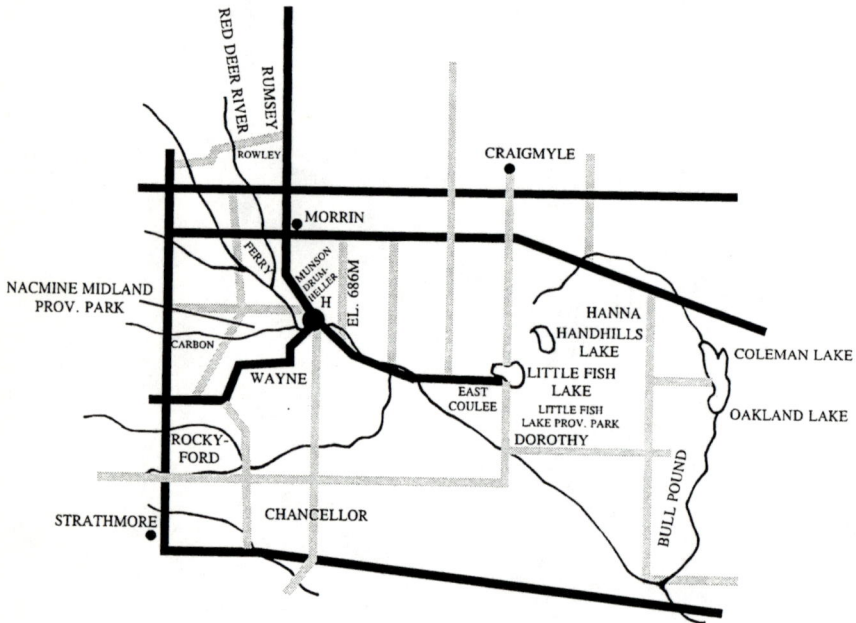

RED DEER RIVER

RUMSEY

ROWLEY

CRAIGMYLE

MORRIN

FERRY

MUNSON DRUM-HELLER

H

EL. 686M

NACMINE MIDLAND PROV. PARK

CARBON

HANNA

HANDHILLS LAKE

COLEMAN LAKE

WAYNE

EAST COULEE

LITTLE FISH LAKE

LITTLE FISH LAKE PROV. PARK

OAKLAND LAKE

ROCKY-FORD

DOROTHY

BULL POUND

STRATHMORE

CHANCELLOR

KEY

PAVED ROADS

IMPROVED ROADS

HOSPITAL   H

1974
Introduction to 'The Badlands'

I would never have had the chance to visit 'The Badlands' and Drumheller City in the Red Deer River Valley if it had not been such a nice day.

The people with whom I was staying just 'take off' and go somewhere if the weather was nice and if they did not have many guests staying with them – there was only myself at this particular time.

I had never seen this type of geological formation before and it was with great interest that I viewed it on such a vast scale.

Therefore, it was quite easy to express myself on paper for all to read, the vastness of this valley was really awe inspiring and to think that it was millions of years old too!

'The Badlands'

Standing on the edge of a ridge
I gazed down upon
Hundreds of strange looking rocks
In a Valley, known
As The Dinosaur Valley.

There are two canyons in this valley,
Horsethief Canyon and Horseshoe Canyon.
Horsethief Canyon is indeed inspiring to see,
For many tons of petrified marine life
And fossils can be found.

Horseshoe Canyon is located on
Highway number nine
And is horseshoe shaped
As seen from the air.
There are no roads leading into or out of this
    Canyon.

Nothing grows in these Canyons
Except dried-up grass,
But, there are a few shrubs and bushes
On top of the prairie or ridge
Plus yellow grass.

The rocks have been called many things
Over the years –
'Hoodoos', 'Voodoos',
Or 'The Badlands'
Which meant something evil,

Or conjured up a vivid picture
Of Cowboys and Indians
With guns, bows and arrows
Chasing after each other
Over the rugged plains.

But, it is not at all evil,
Or anything to do with the Western myths,
Just barren and interesting historical,
And geological formations
Where rocks have erupted from the ground

Like volcanoes, with indented tops,
And, with strange encrustments
Around their edges.
I tried to get down for a closer look,
And found I was not the only one to be so
    curious

For there were several tourists
All of the same mind.
The rocky edge was crumbling,
So safety came first.
I climbed halfway down,

Then stopped, beside a rock
And sat for a while, looking around,
It was very hot in the mid-day sun
And the sky was bright blue
With scudding cloud.

My eyes closed in the heat
And I semi-drowsed,
To be woken suddenly!
By a sudden sting on my arm.
Something had come out of the long grass.

Wide awake, I looked down at my arm
To see it swelling alarmingly.
A big fly sat sunning itself
On the same rock where I sat –

It looked like a horsefly to me
That had done the damage.
I stood up hastily, trying to kill it,
But it flew off, to bite someone else
And inflict pain.

I climbed further down
And was joined by a friend
(We had agreed to meet somewhere),
But, I did not think it would be there!
We climbed down to the floor of the canyon

Feeling so small against the height
Of the rocks.
My friend told me that these were
Known as Petrified Rocks,
Caused by a great inland sea

Inundating Drumheller
Millions of years ago
Causing marine life to exist
In the Red Deer River Valley.
Erosion came

And, the encrusted rocks were revealed.
All sorts of interesting fossils
Have been found here,
The most common,
Being the oyster shell.

Sometimes, you can be lucky enough
To find a real pearl inside.
The area we visited was known as
'The Oyster Beds'.

We were joined by other people
Brave enough to scramble down
And we all looked around
For petrified oyster shells.
I was lucky enough to find one intact.

We held our breath as I struggled to
Open the shell and found, a genuine
Pearl inside much to my great delight.
Alas, I had to leave it there
Amidst the rest of the marine life.

Towards the end of our trip,
We visited the
'Largest Little Church in the World',
Seating six people at a time,
And many thousands in a year.

The church was built in 1957
Especially for those who wished to meditate
As they toured the trail.
We toured the museum at Drumheller City
And saw a thirty foot long

Edmontosarus Skeleton of the
Duck Billed Dinosaur – one of the many
Skeletons unearthed
From the hills of the Red Deer River Valley
And a skull of Pachyrhinosarus and interesting
    fossils.

After the museum visit,
We drove by car along Dinosaur Trail,
Down to the Munson Ferry
Where cars are carried across the river
By cable ferry

To the Dinosaur Graveyard,
Where a complete skeleton
Was excavated from its resting place
Of several million years, and is
Now lying in the museum at Ottawa.

As we met up with our friends
In the nearby car park.
Our day ended on a humorous note.
Collecting the car from the park,
My friend's brother reversed

To get the car out of the park.
Unfortunately, we were so busy talking
That he forgot to look where he was going
And backed right into a high
Grass-covered bank with a thud.

We shuddered to a stop
Wondering why the car suddenly
Became filled with fumes.
We stepped out of the car,
One by one
And looked around.
A large wad of earth and grass
Had become rammed down the 'muffler'[3]
Which caused a laugh.
This took considerable time to unblock,

---

[3] 'Muffler' is the silencer of a motor vehicle [N. Amer.] sometimes confused with the exhaust pipe.

But, at last, we were on our way again,
After a really exciting day,
Which would remain with me
Over the ensuing years.

1974

Introduction to the Summer Cottage Near Caroline in North-West Alberta

The cottage was in a beautiful spot surrounded by nature of all sorts and on a hot July day with a slight breeze, the waving grasses and wildflowers, dragonflies and birds presented a charming sight.

From the outside, the cottage did not show the disaster that had occurred to it inside. It was indeed a pity that nothing could be done to repair the damage – but, it would only happen again.

There was nothing much I could do to help, so I just sat in the long grass, watching nature in peace. I wish now, that I had taken some pictures of the Summer Cottage.

My memories are of the sweetly scented wildflowers and especially of the dragonflies and the drone of the bees.

Location of the Summer Cottage – 3 Miles North-East and 2 Miles East of Caroline in North-West Alberta

(Sketch Map, not to scale)

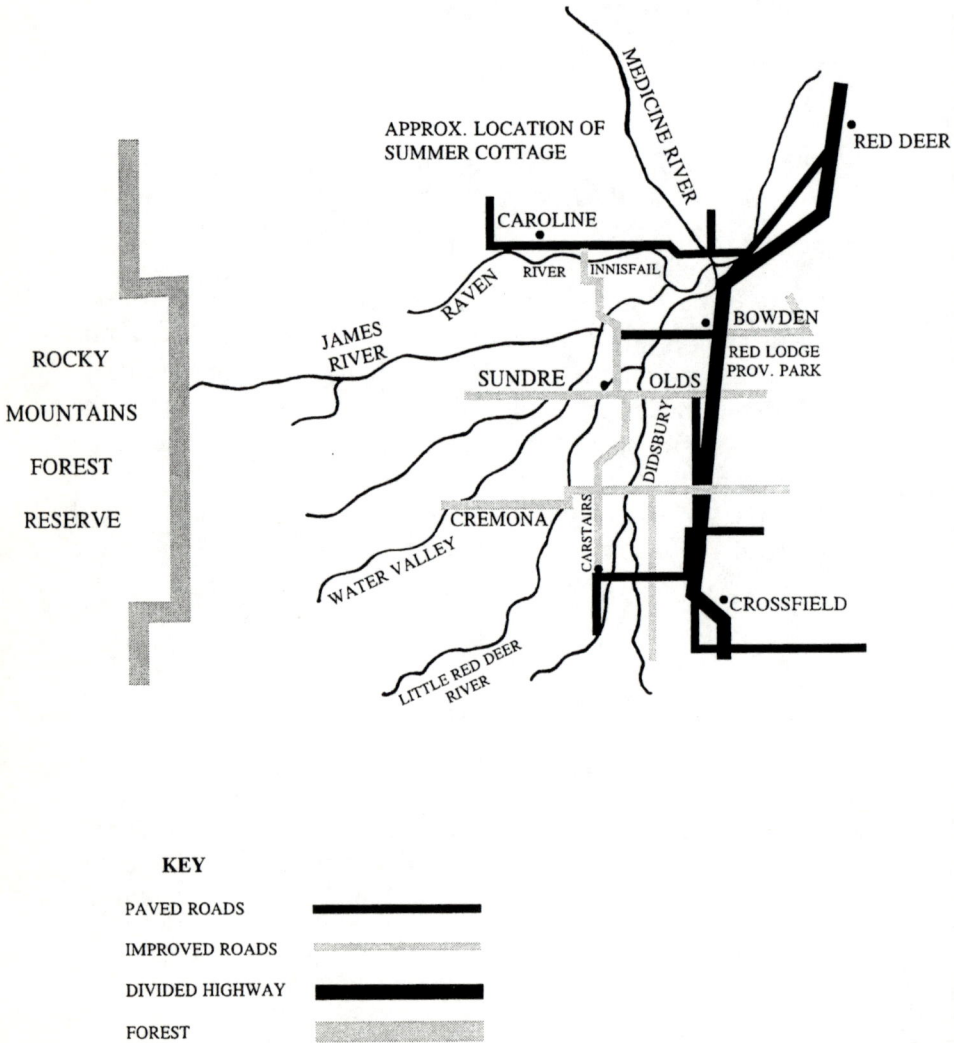

The Summer Cottage

The day looked promising
With clear skies
And brightly shining sun.

We left at nine-thirty in the morning,
Taking a picnic lunch,
Passing through Balzac;

Stopping at Airdrie,
Visiting a saddle shop,
Looking at leather goods, jackets and saddles.

We passed on, through Crossfield,
Carstairs, Didsbury, Olds and Innisfail,
Finally, turning west to Raven Station,

A government operated fish hatchery
In a provincial park.
Unfortunately, it was closed,

So we had our lunch at a picnic table
Underneath the tall pine trees,
With squirrels and chipmunks

Waiting for the crumbs to fall
Then, shyly creeping up to grasp the food,
Retreating to the trees to eat their spoils.

I noticed the pine trees were covered
With a thick white cotton-like substance
Which had a yellowish-brown shell within.

Breaking one open, I found a small
Moth-like insect inside
Which wriggled, giving off a horrible smell.

My friend told me
That these insects were
Killing the poor pine trees.

We cleared the picnic table
Then left for
The summer cottage which was about

Fifteen miles from Caroline,
And I saw some really beautiful scenery
On the way,

Consisting of mustard and flax fields
In bright yellows and blues,
Making the countryside similar to a quilt.

There were poplar and pine trees;
Prairie flowers and heather;
And, in places, the ground was very dry.

We drove off the gravelled road,
Turning right, over two fields
And through a gate.

Everywhere looked overgrown,
But, in the midst of all this,
Was the outline of a small cottage

Painted white, with a small porch
Over the front door.
A sweet perfume filled the air

Being a combination of the grass, trees
And wildflowers in the meadows close by.
Wild, white sweet smelling clover

Grew, about four feet high.
Poplar and pine trees filled the land in
    abundance,
And lots of black dragonflies

With four wings and long bodies
Flew everywhere.
I have never seen so many of these insects before!

Two old barns were built
On land near the cottage
And housed all sorts of things,

Including the contents of the
Summer cottage by the look of it.
I wonder why?

The barns were well-built,
About forty years old,
But one of them was leaning.

Likely, a gale force wind could
Easily blow it down, one day
If the buildings were not restored.

Nearby were some wooden buildings,
Nothing special to look at,
But my friends stayed there

When they came for a weekend,
For the summer cottage
Was not what it used to be.

Some time ago, the combination of
Heavy rains and a stream
At the bottom of the garden

Made the water rise
And flood the ground underneath the
    basement
Where there was no outlet.

So the waters rose higher
Flooding the cottage,
Which made the floor collapse

Into the basement
Taking the furniture with it!
A lot of the items were moved

To the barns;
And the purpose of this visit
Was to salvage more things out of the cottage;

Preserve the iron stove
By cleaning off the rust, and oiling -
The stove burnt wood and baked excellent bread -

And move the stove to the nearby wooden building
Where my friends spend occasional weekends
During summer and winter months.

I noticed a nest of swallows in the
Corner of the room against the door frame
About six feet high.

There were three tiny birds
In the nest
Looking so sweet.

We left the cottage, with its floor on a slope,
Having done everything
To remove objects of use,

And went to the wooden building nearby
Which was built off the ground on stilts,
So it was quite a steep climb

To the front door,
But it was better to have it so high
Than to experience flooding.

It was quite nice inside.
All the shelves were fully stocked
With china, glassware and cutlery.

There were tinned provisions,
No running water –
This was fetched from the stream –

A stove for cooking on
And a gas-operated heater for winter months
Or, when it became extra cold during summer

Was available, when required.
There were two bedrooms – one for a guest –
And bedclothes

They usually brought with them
To avoid getting damp and musty
From lack of use.

There used to be a raging torrent of water
At the bottom of the second field,
But, during the course of the years,

It has faded,
And is now a mere trickle of water
Amidst marshy land.

Soon, it was time to leave.
I do not suppose that I will have
A chance to return

To the summer cottage
With its painted walls
And sloping floor

All overgrown and forlorn.
So I took a last look round
And will remember for ever

The sweet smells of the countryside
Away from the polluted city,
Dusty roads and noisy cars.

We drove back through Caroline,
Which is a very small town,
But it had eight wheatpools[4]

And a community centre,
Where we stopped and went inside
To see their Indoor Stampede Centre.

From there, we went through Balzac,
Which had three wheatpools
At that time, and

---

[4]   A 'wheatpool' in Canada is where harvested grain is stored until required for flour
or cattle fodder.

One Post Office-cum-general store;

A nearby railway siding,

A few houses here and there, and that was all.

I was glad to return to the Ranch

As the day had been hot and tiring,

But I would not forget my trip

TO THE SUMMER COTTAGE.

(1874) 1974

Introduction to the Town of Fort Macleod

I originally met my friend in the city of Calgary at the local ramblers club. I cannot quite remember when, but unfortunately, over the years since my visit to Fort Macleod, I have lost touch with her. Her father had a farm in Southern Alberta (where the climate is very hot and the chores have to be done early in the morning before the sun is high in the sky).

I recall her father was a very nice man and did his best on that hot, dry land.

I was glad to have had the opportunity to accept the invitation to stay with them that year and enjoy their hospitality.

I enjoyed visiting the reconstruction of the Fort, the original one being built in 1874, for there was much of interest to see.

Besides the town of Fort Macleod, we visited several other interesting places in the near vicinity, and I was so glad that I had taken time to do so, for I am sure that I will never have a chance to return.

Town of Fort Macleod

Location: southern Alberta

I have heard so much about
The town of Fort Macleod
And was looking forward to my visit
At the beginning of August.

It was quite an old town,
The original Fort being established in 1874.
A replica of that first Fort
Was constructed, then opened on 4th July 1959.

I left Calgary city on the bus
At twelve-thirty, and arrived at Fort Macleod
About three in the afternoon.
My friend, and her father, met me.

Glancing around the bus depot,
All I could see, at that time,
Were drunken Indians lying around,
Or fighting, and young Indian children playing;

And, so much litter lying everywhere,
I thought it quite a shame.
The streets looked very much
Like an old western town,

With wooden sidewalks –
Where you could imagine
Cowboys once walked with spurs jingling,
Or guns cocked.

There were wooden rails outside
Most of the buildings
Where a horse or two
Could be tethered –

The hotel looked like a saloon
And very authentic too,
With its swinging entrance doors
Which reminded me of the old western days

Of long ago.
A sign, depicting the name
Of the hotel,
Swung to and fro in the strong wind,

With eerie, rusty, squeaking noises,
But it was lovely and cosy inside,
And I seem to remember seeing,
A huge oil painting of the man

Whom the town was named after,
Hanging in prominent position
High above, on the wall.
We stayed awhile

In this old saloon,
Enjoying the atmosphere
And listening to conversation
Humming all around us.

Then we left,
To look at the Fort
Filled with interesting museum pieces
And relics of early life.

Within the Fort itself
Were reconstructions of a blacksmith's shop
With equipment used in those early
Days of long ago, by ranchers;

A chapel,
Where the atmosphere of the pioneer church
Has been restored
For worshippers of the present century;

An Office of Law was reconstructed
On the same site as the original Law Office,
Which was built in 1884,
And the atmosphere felt just right;

A medical building
Where early dentists and doctors
Made their mark in the 'Old West',
And some of their equipment, was on display;

A kitchen, has been reconstructed
With early pioneer utensils,
And cooking information,
For those interested in experimenting;

There is a police museum
Where relics of early times, uniforms,
Weapons and pictures of the police
From old western, pioneer days can be viewed.

Finally, we saw colourful Indian tepees,
Including a tepee owned by a chief
Of the Peigan tribe, on display,
Accompanied by souvenirs for the public to buy.

There were a few other things to see,
Including an old Union Jack which
Still flew over the Fort
As it did in the days gone past.

We left the town of Fort Macleod
Homeward-bound,
Leaving marks imprinted on my memory –
The sight of bygone years.

(1903) 1974
Introduction to the Lost Town of Frank

The old lost town of Frank really made me feel nostalgic. I had read a great deal about the tragedy before I visited the area, but certainly did not expect to experience such a depth of feeling when I actually went to the area. (It was almost as though I had known the townsfolk who used to live there.)

In fact, my feelings were so strong that I felt I just had to write something about this town, or village as it was known locally.

I have never felt this way before about any place I visited – possibly it was because so many people perished, buried for ever beneath the pile of rocks.

Lost Town of Frank

Location: Crows Nest Pass Valley, southern Alberta

It was sheer chance
That I visited the town of Frank.
I had read and heard
A great deal about the rock slide
Which had overtaken the village in 1903,
Wanting to see for myself
The site of the event.

My friend's uncle
Had lived under the shadow of Turtle Mountain,
But, fortunately, had got away
Before the rock slide,
And I have not met anyone
Connected with Frank
Who could have given me any information.

There is a provincial signpost
Which has been erected
On the site of Frank,
Which was once, a small, busy, mining town,
And is now a heap of boulders
With no houses in sight.
Regretfully, most of the houses,

And inhabitants,
Are buried beneath the rocks.
Very few escaped
The wrath of the falling mountain.
People say that the mining operations
Which penetrated Turtle Mountain, some 1,000ft
Helped to cause the mammoth disaster.

I experienced quite an eerie feeling
As I paused to look at the remains of Frank.
I could almost hear the shouts of people
Trying to escape the rock slide.
In fact, I could definitely feel 'something' present,
And a kind of sadness pervaded the whole area
Where once there was happiness and joy.

Has anyone else experienced the same feeling?
I glanced over the huge boulder piles
As far as my eyes could see,
Vainly searching for something to break the
    horizon,
There was nothing, and not even a twig moved.
I lingered a little longer,
Something forcing me to stay.

Then, turning myself away,
I climbed into the car
With much regret,
My feelings confused
And my whole being saddened
By that tragedy
Of so many years ago.

1975

Introduction to my Alberta and Calgary Recollections

In these following few verses I have remembered the fun of the past and some new topics as well.

The day of the Annual Barbecue, I recall that someone, be it boy or man, blocked up the vent of the bee hives and prevented the insects from coming out and going about their business of pollen collecting, for the purpose of making honey. Some of the poor things had suffocated before help came along, not often were the hives checked to see that all was well.

At the Midway, I recall my friends and I boarded one of those fast-moving pieces of machinery that go round at least a hundred times a minute, and when we stepped off, we were still going round and collapsed into a heap on the ground!

My Alberta and Calgary Recollections

Locations: various – throughout Alberta and the city of Calgary

My July visit was uneventful
As nothing exciting occurred,
But it is full of interesting recollections
Worthy of notation.

It usually takes me a few days to settle
Down to Canadian timing changes,
And this year was no exception.
I stayed at the usual ranch,

Catching up with local gossip.
The beginning of July was hot and dry,
And we had a party of Lithuanians
Camping in the grounds of the ranch

For their Annual Barbecue;
At the same time,
An American party arrived from Spokane
In order to attend the Stampede

The following day, at Calgary.
A big wind blew up after dinner that night
And the hot land grew cold.
The next day, 7th July

We saw a spectacular lightning storm
Followed by thunder and heavy rain
Which cleared by about eight in the morning,
Enabling us to go downtown

To 9th Avenue and view the Stampede Parade.
However, my best Stampede Parade
Was viewed on my first visit to
Calgary in 1972.

As the years have rolled by,
That first parade has remained in my mind,
For the others I have seen
Do not seem to be the same.

On another evening,
Some friends and myself
Visited the exhibition grounds
Of the Calgary Stampede,

And looked at photographs, oil paintings,
Artists painting portraits on the spot,
All sorts of handicrafts made by Indians,
Maybe some by Eskimos?

We went to look at some farming implements
So different from English standards,
And we saw a model of Calgary city.
There was a Midway too, which we all enjoyed.

Before buying some refreshments
And making our way to the Grandstand
To view the Chuckwagon Races
Which began at 7.45 p.m. until 9 p.m.,

Followed by the Grandstand Show;
We met the rest of our friends
And walked back to the Midway
To have our fun.

At eleven there were the beautiful fireworks
Which we all enjoyed to the full.
Walking back along the Midway[5]
To the front gates,

We boarded the special buses
In the bus park
Which would take us in all directions
Across the city of Calgary, homeward-bound.

During this July visit
I was awakened many times
At about three in the morning, by coyotes
Calling their mates.

It seemed to me, to be a comforting sound.
My friend of the past, who used
To look after the horses on the ranch,
Had left to go to the university,

---

[5]   'Midway' is the Canadian expression for Fair – Fun Fair.

And to this day, I have seen her no more,
Although I often think of her and wish
She would get in touch.
So, there was a new young lady at the ranch

Looking after the horses,
But it was not the same as with my friend,
And I felt so lonely without her.
We still went on adventurous horse rides,

But, somehow, it was not the same.
I met another friend one night
And we went out for a meal downtown
To the steak bar;

We started with cocktails,
Followed by a huge side dish of salads
Of every description, including fruits
Which were really quite delicious.

But you had to be careful
To leave enough room for the lovely steaks
And especially, the jacket potatoes,
With that extra special serving of soured cream!

I was quite impressed with the steak bar.
It was built of pinewood and carpet throughout,
With dimly lit lights from the ceiling,
And candles on every table,

With red serviettes.
There were alcoves along the walls,
Hanging from the walls and ceilings
Were copperware antiques

Of a life which existed
Some years ago.
After our dinner,
We visited a movie theatre

So, finishing the evening off with a good film –
It was only three dollars in those days!
Then we went to our respective buses,
Homeward-bound.

Another day, a small party of us
Gathered at the ranch,
Then made our way to the bus stop
On our way downtown to the zoo.

It was a nice hot day and we had a lot of fun.
Returning home,
We stopped at one of the big stores
And I bought a Canadian beechwood

Salad bowl set –
A lovely memento of my visit.
On another day,
We had quite an adventure

When the bull broke out of the corral.
We tried to chase it back,
But it broke the fence,
And eluded us!

We were all running about in circles
Vainly trying to miss the bull,
Fortunately, none of us was
Wearing the bright colour of red!

Eventually, the man of the ranch
Threw a rope and it snaked across his neck
Encapturing him quite tightly,
But, by this time, he was so enraged

That the rope snapped,
And he was off again,
But, he forgot where he was,
And the corral gate shut behind him with a bang!

Some puppies were brought in one night
By relatives from Caroline.
They were cute Blue Heeler Puppies,
(I had never seen that breed before)

They were put in the barn
To keep them from harm.
During the next two or three days
My friends and I went to two rodeos,

One at Innisfail and the other
At Carstairs.
The best rodeo, I thought,
Was at Carstairs

Where there was a parade.
After the parade,
We bought tickets
For the grandstand,

And sat high up from the ground
Away from all the dust.
It was a very hot day, and we all
Became very sunburnt.

Before I left Alberta this time,
I had many more horse riding sessions
Across the beautiful countryside,
And I also went shopping downtown many times;

Buying good quality Canadian corduroy
Plus linen fabric
To take home with me.
My only regret is that I was overweight at

The airport, and was out of cash
So could not pay excess baggage,
But, luck was on my side, and I took
It all with me, leaving behind my Bank Account
    Code.

1975–1977

Introduction to Lake Louise

Lake Louise is a beautiful place to visit, but I prefer it all to myself really, for in the summer months, the place is alive with tourists of all shapes and sizes, eating sandwiches, ice creams and drinking cans of beer or flavoured sodas.

I visited Lake Louise on my own in the late spring, which was preferable, as I enjoyed the magnificent beauty of the lake in silence; and also, with a friend in the height of summer.

Visiting the lake on my own offered much scope in the wildlife I managed to see during the period of time I wandered up and down the lakeshores.

Lake Louise is well worth a visit as it is a most picturesque spot, really, at any time of the year, and I recommend the area as an excellent stopping-off place for tourists.

Lake Louise

Location: Banff National Park, north-west of Calgary

I stood on the snow edged banks
Of Lake Louise in late spring,
Gazing across the rippling waters
At the white snows
Lying by the base of the mountains
On the other side of the lake.

The hour was early yet
And I wanted to be alone
With my dreams and thoughts.
Everywhere was still and quiet
With no tourists abroad –
Exactly how I liked it.

I breathed in the fresh, cold air
Laden with the smell of snow
And noticed wisps of cloud
Hovering near the mountainside.
A sudden squawking broke the silence.
Looking up, I saw two birds

Fighting on the lake over a titbit.
They sank out of sight,
Beneath the waters
Still squabbling,
And, finally, drifted downlake together
In peace.

The lake looked greyish-blue
In the morning light,
And the centre mountains reflecting the snows
Appeared a purple-grey;
Light traces of snow lay on surrounding mountains,
But I could clearly see the fir trees

Now unaffected by the snows.
A thin layer of ice
Still floated on the lake
And reflected the still grey sky
Which promised more snow.
Nothing moved,

For there was not even
A breeze stirring in the trees.
I turned, and walked further
Along the lakeshore,
Kicking the stones with my feet,
Feeling the snow in my hands

As I crawled over a fallen log
And sat on the edge
To reminisce about the other time
I visited Lake Louise[6] –
When the sun was high in the sky
And there were many tourists around.

The grass was green, and the
Lake, reflecting a gorgeous blue
From the skies;
There were scattered flowers here and there
And the small fleecy clouds curled around
The mountainsides –

I came to with a start,
Feeling very cold.
Small flecks of white
Fell down out of the leaden skies,
A slight shower at first,
And then, faster and thicker

Until the log where I was sitting
Became covered in snow,
And my footsteps leading across the shores
Were filled with snow.
Soon, there was nothing to show
Where I had walked,

Only a vast whiteness

---

[6]   A picture of Lake Louise can be seen on the back cover of this book.

Covered the land
As far as the eye could see.
It was obvious that I had to go
Back to the warmth of my hotel
And to the present, instead of the past.

1977

Introduction to Dry Island Buffalo Jump Provincial Park

This area is very interesting to visit, especially if you have not seen cactus growing in great profusion before, and such tiny ones at that – the cactus covered the grounds of the Red Deer River Valley in a green, prickly mass.

I saw fossilised buffalo bones lying on the ground in numerous places and if we had been able to spare a day or two there, I would have liked to have been bold enough to venture to the bottom of the river bed and see if I could find some Indian artefacts – these would have to be given in to the park rangers or left where they were (a difficult decision to make when I was interested in this sort of thing).

It was fun wandering along the banks of the river with nothing in particular to do.

All too soon, it was time to leave – if I can make a return visit, I will.

Location of Dry Island Buffalo Jump Provincial Park at Elnora, East of Huxley, in Alberta

(Sketch Map, not to scale)

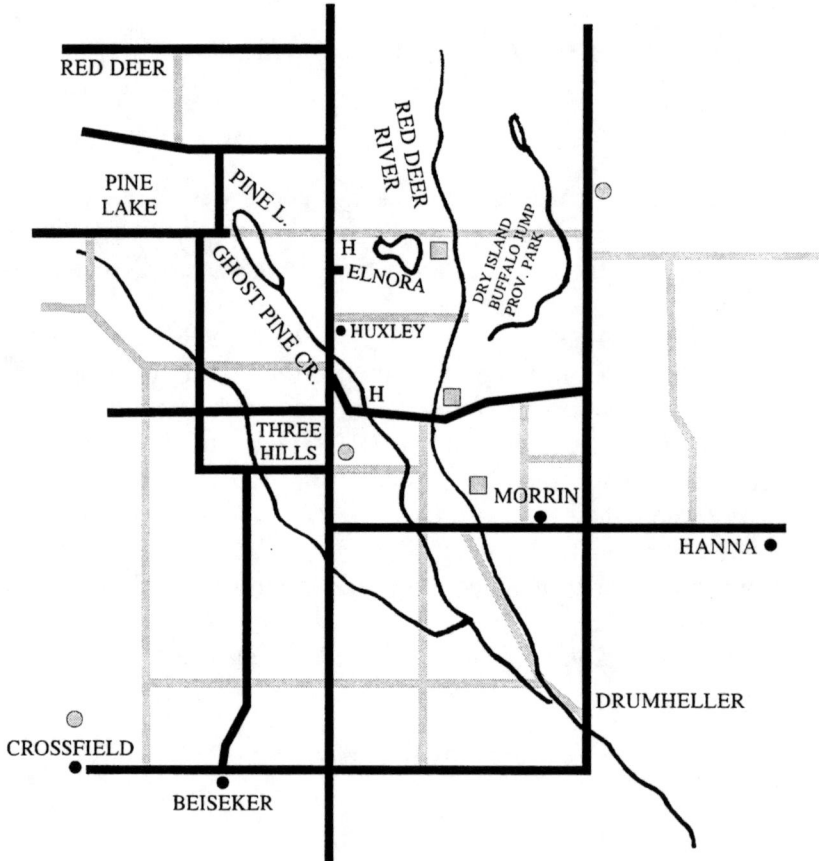

RED DEER

PINE LAKE

PINE L.

RED DEER RIVER

GHOST PINE CR.

H
ELNORA

DRY ISLAND BUFFALO JUMP PROV. PARK

HUXLEY

H

THREE HILLS

MORRIN

HANNA

DRUMHELLER

CROSSFIELD

BEISEKER

KEY

PAVED ROADS

IMPROVED ROADS

FED. AND PROV.

H   HOSPITAL

Dry Island Buffalo Jump
Provincial Park

I had always wanted to visit
This National Park
In the Red Deer River Valley,
Where a fantastic view can be seen
From the cliff tops,

Across a two mile wide, and
One thousand feet deep canyon,
Which has been carved out by
The Red Deer River flowing
Over dinosaur bearing beds.

Glacier erosion has taken place
Over many thousands of years,
And is similar to the 'Badlands' of Drumheller.
The Red Deer River Valley
Dates back millions of years

To the prehistoric era,
Then, later, to the days
When buffalo covered the plains,
And Indians used to drive buffalo
Over the cliffs to their deaths –
Hence the name of Buffalo Jump National
     Provincial Park –

The meat and skins of the buffalo
Being collected by Indians,
For food and clothing.
There are still fossilised buffalo bones
To be found on the grounds

Amidst tiny cacti and tall fir trees.
Dinosaur bones and Indian artefacts
Can still be found at the bottom of
The Red Deer River if you are patient enough
To spare time for a search.

My friend and I had two hours spare,
So we wandered along the river's edge,
Our feet springing on the cactus covered grounds,
Finding the atmosphere peaceful
And the countryside, picturesque.

We saw no one during that time,
But, I had that strange feeling
We were being watched
By someone, unseen –
Perhaps a buffalo? or maybe, an Indian!

1977

Introduction to the Round-Up

The round-up was a lot of fun. Unfortunately, the photographs that were taken with my camera, did not come out as there was something wrong with the lens, and the photographs were all too light – you could just about see my outline and that was all!

I was shouted at several times by the rancher of our vacation ranch to keep myself under control and not to rush the cattle otherwise we would have a stampede on our hands! Being so keen, I found it hard to follow his advice, but found it paid off in the end!

Experiencing a round-up first hand was something that not many visitors have the chance to participate in, and it is certainly best not to say no, as another chance will not be forthcoming so quickly.

Oh, we thoroughly enjoyed every minute of our adventures – I just wished it could have lasted longer.

The Round-Up

Location: A ranch near Balzac

A neighbouring rancher
Wanted some help
To round up his cattle.

He wanted the cattle
Brought from a distant ranch
To his own.

Having no help,
Other than the odd hand or two,
He contacted the rancher

At the vacation ranch
Where my friend and I were staying.
We had never encountered the opportunity

To take part in a round-up before,
And had only seen such events on television.
So it was a wonderful chance for us.

We saddled our horses and collected our lariats.
I gave my camera to the rancher's wife,
With instructions to photograph us

Rounding-up the cattle
As we rode past
In an hour or two.

Off we went,
The three of us, on our horses
Down the drive, turning northwards.

Upon arrival at the neighbour's ranch
We were shown how to cut out the cattle
From the milling bunch

Gathered high on a ridge
Of the rolling hills,
Looking down on to the ranch below.

The task looked easy enough to me,
But it was only when I tried to do it
That I found out how hard it was!

I managed to cut them out
From the main bunch,
But just could not keep them from straying.

The television westerns
Made rounding-up cattle
Look so easy,

But, oh dear, it was very hard!
Finally, I had my bunch under control
As had everyone else.

And we moved off
In groups of four or six people
Driving about twenty cattle in a bunch

Down the sides of the roads.
Fortunately, not much traffic
Passed this way,

For we were clearly here to stay.
It was fun driving them along,
And keeping an eye

On the strays,
That kept wanting to wander
Away from the main bunch.

It was hard work for my horse
To keep them together,
Especially as we were

At the head of them all.
We passed our ranch
Within the hour,

And photographs were duly taken
Of each, and every one of us;
So at least I could say

I had helped at a round-up.
Eventually, we arrived at our destination,
But the difficult part had just begun!

We had to cut out five cows
From each bunch for branding
And the rest were penned in the corrals.

Each of the five cows we had to cut out
Of the bunch, had cuts in their ears
To distinguish them from the others.

It would be quite easy to separate
The cows from the main bunch,
But, quite difficult to corral them singly

As the others would want to come out
At the same time as I put each cow in.
This was overcome by the rancher,

Who had made an irreversible chute
Leading to each corral
Which would prevent cattle already penned

From escaping, to mingle with the others.
I soon finished cutting my bunch,
And guided my horse away from the scene.

We had no plans for branding,
Leaving that for the specialists
From another ranch.

Soon, we all gathered in the ranch kitchen
For a welcome cup of coffee
After our exertions.

Then, taking a final look at the cattle,
We remounted our horses
Making our way southwards towards our vacation
  ranch.

1978–1979

Introduction to my Winter Visit to Alberta

If my Canadian friend had not decided to get married during January, I would never have had the opportunity to pay a winter visit to Alberta, but I was glad I did, despite the cold and the few hardships suffered: it was a trip not to be forgotten in a hurry.

It always looks so different in winter than it does during the summer months. I saw people skiing along the roadsides of Calgary city, which, of course, we do not see at home; the ice-packed pavements were the downfall of many a careless footed person and the icy north-east wind blowing was a real 'killer' to me. The temperatures dropped very low whilst I was there, and everything froze up. There was not much snow on the ground at the time, and although there were some snow flurries, there was nothing serious to keep me snowbound, but I nearly suffered frostbite by waiting too long on a street corner for some friends!

257

Part I

Winter Season

Locations: Balzac, Bassano, and the city of Calgary

In Alberta, the climate is very dry,
So unlike England
Where the damp cold
Penetrates your bones,
And makes you feel bitterly cold.

I was in Alberta
One winter season a few years ago
Visiting friends – my mother said
It was a mistake, for it was so cold!
Knowing what a cold mortal I was.

I stayed on a farm a few miles
North of Calgary,
Far away from the bustling city,
Preferring the peace
Of the surrounding countryside.

It had been a beautiful October day
The sun rose high in the sky
And it became really hot –
Hot enough to obtain a suntan.
As yet, we had not experienced

A really hard frost,
But this particular night,
I had an invitation
To attend the auditorium
For a Senior Citizens' Choral Show.

I set off, with two friends
Whilst it was still light.
The sky was very clear,
But there was no indication
That we were to have frost that night.

The choral show was very entertaining,
And lasted a good hour or two.
When we came out
We were surprised to see
A heavy hoar frost over everything.

We had to sit in the car
With the heater on and engine running
To try and clear the frost
From the windscreen
In order to see where we were going.

It was a long time
Before the windscreen
Was cleared of frost,
And we were able to
Drive home safely.

My friends said it felt very cold,
But I, thought not.
Everywhere was white –
Trees in peoples' gardens, and
The once green grass;

Overhead hydro lines;[7]
Roads and sidewalks.
It was a very bright, moonlight night,
With stars twinkling,
Frost glistening, and sparkling all around.

We soon left the city behind,
And drove along the country lanes
So dark and cold.
There was little wind blowing –
The only sound, was us,

Moving along the road,
Leaving our tyre tracks as
We drove on into the night,
The lights of
City streets vanishing as we sped onwards.

I would love
To have left the car,
And walked up the frost-covered roads
Along grass verges
To the farm.

---

[7]   'Hydro Lines' is the Canadian wording for overhead electricity cables.

For there is nothing
I like better
Than to walk alone
On a bright, moonlight night,
And to smell the sweet night air;

So refreshing from the smell
Of oil and fumes in a big city.
The car drew into the drive,
And the lady of the house
Stepped out of the car, and,

I followed,
Closing the door of the house
Carefully, and quietly behind me.
All was still, except for night sounds,
In the yard beyond.

I climbed the stairs to my bed
And looked out, over the fields
So bright
With the light of the moon,
To reminisce.

Part II
The Wedding

In January
When temperatures can drop to forty below
My friend married.
It was a lovely day,
And the skies so steely blue
With a pale sun,
Threw shadows on to the sparse snows.

Her dress was virgin white
With a gathered frill at the bottom.
Her veil, and sleeves,
A floating, frothy white,
And her bouquet was of
Roses, orange-red and white,
With everlasting flowers.

There were three bridesmaids,
In short-sleeved dresses,
Of pastel orange, orange-red
And brown,
Each with a flower in her hair
And carrying a matching bouquet.

The bridegroom, his ushers,
And best man,
Were dressed in suits
Of a dark brown,
With frilled shirts
Matching the colourful
Bridesmaids dresses.

The church was warm,
And still decorated with
Christmas festivities.
The guests arrived,
Shivering, in their best clothes,
Treading across the snow
In delicate shoes.

I wore a long, pale blue,
Bonded dress,
Carrying gold sandals and
Bag in my hands,
Complete with fur coat and hood,
To keep out the cold.
A Canadian wedding

Was a new experience for me.
How I enjoyed all the activities
Over the past week!
Including the dress rehearsal
And the last minute details,
Such as paper flowers for the cars
With fervent prayers for a dry day.

Before the ceremony started,
Both bride and groom's parents,
Each led their son and daughter
To the altar,
Where they joined together
Before the priest
To commence their vows.

This was something new for me,
As no English wedding
Was quite like this.
The ceremony over, we left for the
Church Hall a short distance away,
To enjoy the reception
And meet the other guests.

The bride and groom,
Plus entourage,
Left for the studio
To have their photographs taken
For posterity.
They joined the reception
In time for dinner,

Which was a lovely meal.
Afterwards,
The cake was cut,
And it was time for the
Toasts and speeches.
All out-of-town guests,

Had to stand up
And be identified!
An overwhelming experience
To be viewed
By over one hundred guests!
Each guest sank down relieved,
Hoping to sink into oblivion!

The tables were pushed back
For the dancing to start.
There was no shortage
Of partners

For the English girl,
Who was in much demand
And only too pleased to dance the whole
    night away.

All too soon,
The bride and groom
Made their way
To the waiting car,
Taking them away to change
Before coming back
To make fond farewells

To their friends, parents and relations.
And, then, at long last,
To the waiting car they went,
Followed by everyone
Waiting to see the fun.
There were old tin cans
And, 'Just Married' signs too.

Off they went,
Accompanied by the blaring of horns
And shouts of
"Good luck"
To their honeymoon
On a distant island
With considerable heat.

The guests departed
One by one,
Leaving family and close friends,
To clear away the débris
Of the most exciting day

To be experienced, not only by
Bride and groom,
But by all those involved.

We were homeward-bound
In the early hours of twilight,
Over the crisp white snow
Which scrunched under
Our wheels.
We turned into the drive,
And put the car away, for another day.

Part III
Afternoon and Evening Walk

Despite the temperatures being
At least forty degrees below
I was fortunate that it did not snow.
There was sparse snow on the ground,
But you could see the drive,
And the hill beyond the farm
From which the snow had blown.

The trees were bare of leaf,
And where the wind had
Blown the snow away,
You could see the grass
Coloured brown, instead of green
By the intense cold and
Continual frosts.

It was late afternoon,
And, the sun had set.
A pale, faint half moon
Had risen
High into the darkening skies,
A few stars were out,
And shadows were flung

Across the drive,
By the light, so high, on a nearby pole
Standing in earth on the lawn.
There were shadows of the fir trees
On the white walls of the farm,
Moving gently in the breeze,
Like giants taking a walk.

A young man, tall and fair,
Came from the cabin beyond.
Dressed in red checked shirt
And blue jeans,
He walked swiftly across the yard,
And disappeared into the farmhouse,
Where I have spent many happy hours.

Beyond the farmhouse and cabin
To the east,
Lay the barn,
Where the horses in winter live,
Or, roam the land, so free
With their shaggy winter coats
Keeping them warm.

My favourite, a Dartmoor pony,
All black, and very stubborn,
Stood, with several others
In the field behind the leafless hedge.
His breath froze as it left his mouth,
And, icicles hung from his nose,
Mane and underneath his stomach.

The snow was churned up from
Tramping of many hooves,
And hay and straw lay round about.
The moon was full
And its shadows bright,
As I made my way
Back, across the fields,

Horses following.
They followed me to the barn,
Where their food was laid out.
I shut the gate
And wandered on,
Past the truck, filled with fencing, and
Its covering of snow,

Making the scene
Perfect for a picture.
The snow lay deep
By the windbreak trees,
And I stood for awhile
Remembering my dreams
Of a past and present era.

The moon passed behind cloud
All shadows temporarily gone,
It was dark and gloomy,
Except for the white snow,
Peaceful, as the land slumbered on,
Broken by the neigh of a horse and
The low of a cow.

Shadows brightened
As the moon reappeared,
And I continued my walk
Along the south side of the field,
By the naked honeysuckle trees,
Green fir trees, so tall, with perfume
So sweet when the weather was warm.

I paused, and listened,
A night bird, I heard,
And the rustle of a fir tree
As a small animal
Scampered along the branch of a fir.
A soft plop!
As a cone fell off on to the ground.

All was still again,
And I walked on,
Across the lawn in summer,
But in winter, a white mass,
Till I met my friend,
The tall, fair Canadian.
We passed the time of day

For several minutes
Then,
He went on his way
And I went on mine.

Part IV
My Bassano Visit

I visited Bassano
Before my return home,
Being collected from the farm
By my friends,
In their station wagon.

Well wrapped up
We prepared for the three hour trek
Across the wide open
Alberta countryside
Which was bleak in winter

And hot in summer,
To the point where the reservoirs dry up.
There was little snow about,
The wind, having blown most away.
The surrounding countryside

Near the motorways
Being caught by the severe frosts,
Was brown, and looked quite dead.
We swung off the motorway
Into a small, snug township,

Which seemed to have more snow
Than anywhere else I had seen,
Driving past the post office
And one or two shops,
We came to a row of townhouses,

And pulled into the drive
Of the centre townhouse,
Whilst we unpacked.
Once inside,
I was surprised to see

How spacious the rooms were.
My favourite room
Had beautiful oil paintings
All over the walls.
My girlfriend was a marvellous artist

Upon natural things.
The stove was in one corner
Against a background of bricks
Another wall, near the window
Was devoted to all sorts of plants;

A bookcase, filled with good books
Graced another wall
The television, too,
Had its special place;
Adjoining this room

Was the kitchen
Where we ate all our meals,
Which overlooked the
Front of the house.
Stairs led to the top of the house.

The spacious landing
Led me to the lovely bathroom,
And two bedrooms.
The stovepipe from downstairs
Came up into my room

And kept it warm all night through.
Overnight, we had a severe frost
So, the following day,
We decided to try the thickness
Of the ice,

On Bassano Dam,
In the station wagon
Which was built
To withstand rough terrain,
And all types of weather.

It was interesting to see
How attractive the countryside looked
With a severe frost.
The trees and hedges
Were all white and still,

The branches of the willow trees
Just hanging, limply,
Swaying in the slight breeze.
There was no sun
At present

To melt the frost,
In fact, the sky was
Quite overcast,
Seemingly, with the threat of snow.
We reached the dam,

Going the long way around,
So that I could see
A bit of the land.
It was quite steep
Down the banks to the bottom of the dam.

We did wonder
Whether the ice
Would take our weight
Without breaking, or even cracking,
But, it did.

So we heaved sighs
Of heartfelt relief.
We went as close to the dam
As we dared.
Surprisingly enough,

The water falling from the dam
Was not frozen at all,
And the noise was deafening
As the water gushed from the top
Of the dam, hitting the bottom.

The ice, near the falling water
Was non-existent.
We stayed awhile,
Listening to the water,
And the crack, crack,

'Like a bullet from a gun'
Of distant ice breaking up
Under pressure.
A few more minutes sped past,
Then, reluctantly,

We left, the way we had come,
Up the steep banks
And on to the road beyond.
I stayed another day
In Bassano,

And then, alas,
I had to leave.
My friend's husband
Took me down to catch the bus;
I appreciated this,

As the place
Was a transport café,
Full of men and smoke,
And my feelings were of discomfort,
As I was distinctly aware

Of their scrutiny.
At last, the bus arrived, and
I clambered on,
Making sure,
I had a good window seat.

The sky was very overcast,
Looking just like snow.
I waved goodbye,
As we moved off
In a flurry of snow.

The snow fell heavier and faster
As we wended our way
To Calgary.
From time to time,
The bus crawled along

With headlamps blazing.
At one time, I thought
We would not make it,
But we did,
And came into Calgary just after six at night.

I was right downtown,
And, oh, how different
It all looked!
The sidewalks were
Hard packed with ice,

Dangerous too.
How glad I was to have
Worn my non-slip leather fur boots.
"Which way do I go for the bus?"
I asked a man on 4th Avenue.

He did not know.
"I'm only a workman," he said.
"But you are English," he marvelled.
"How have you managed
At this cold time of the year?"

He was very interested in me.
In fact, we held a long conversation,
Standing at the roadside,
Our feet melting patches of hard packed ice.
It was cold standing about,

And I made a move to go.
"It was nice meeting you," he said,
Patting my shoulder,
Then shaking my hand.
"Good luck and a safe journey home!"

With that, he was gone.
I found my bus
And arrived at the farm late evening
In heavy snow,
Which was settling and forming

Quite a covering.
I had two days to go
Before returning home.
That time soon went, and I was
Sadly leaving all my friends for another year.

1980

Introduction to Thanksgiving Weekend

Over the years, I have had the opportunity to be in Canada at all seasons of the year, which is what I have wanted to do. It is difficult to say which is my favourite season, as every one has brought forth an interesting occasion to remember.

I enjoyed visiting Canmore Opera House for the very first time, even though it was a very hot and airless night (with no air conditioning!) to see the portrayal of an old Pioneer Opera.

I had a lot of fun with friends, both old and new, when we went hiking the next day in the Rockies. We were fortunate to have a good, dry day, even though it was a little cold.

On Thanksgiving Day (which is a national holiday in Canada) the weather was cool, but not wet. Everyone celebrates Thanksgiving Day with a huge turkey dinner and lots of fun.

In England, of course, we have The Harvest Supper (but no National Holiday), which is usually celebrated up and down the country in churches by way of Services and Suppers are held in Church Halls – both interesting occasions.

I thoroughly enjoyed my Canadian Thanksgiving Weekend.

Thanksgiving Weekend

*Locations: Calgary, Canmore, and the
Rocky Mountains*

This year the harvest
Yielded high quantities of grain.
In fact, at times, it was difficult
To find storage space for all of it
As quite a lot had to be left on the ground.

As soon as everything
Was safely gathered in
The celebrations started,
Not only in individual homes,
But on a larger scale, in church halls and barns.

My friends, their families and myself,
Celebrated Thanksgiving weekend
By visiting the Opera House
At Heritage Park,
To see a Pioneer Opera.

No air conditioning existed
And the night was very hot,
The seats were uncomfortable,
Going up in the middle,
Probably to prevent people from sleeping!

But the opera was interesting,
And told the story of pioneer days
Long past.
The following day we left for a hike
In the Rocky Mountain regions

Of Mount Eisenhower, now called
Castle Mountains.
We reached the base of the mountain
At noon, and stopped for lunch.
Then we continued up the vertical slope

To the second mountain base and lake.
I could go no further –
It was as much as I could manage.
Some of the others climbed the mountain,
But the rest of us stayed below by the lake.

The scenery was spectacular
And the air cold.
As it was nearing winter season
The grass was brown because of the frosts.
In places, ice had formed on the puddles.

We relaxed, and wandered about until
The others returned, then left the area
At quarter past four in the afternoon after an
Exhilarating day.
I ached all over, but it did not matter,

For it had been such a lovely day.
Monday, 13th October was Thanksgiving Day
And a national holiday.
The weather was cool and slightly sunny.
Thanksgiving Day is celebrated

In a special way.
There may be a Square Dance
In a gaily decorated church hall
Followed by a buffet or sit-at-table-meal –
I recall the scene quite well,

Long tables covered in red and white checked
    cloths
Heavily laden with all sorts of food –
I did not stay, as I already had
A dinner invitation at my friend's house, with
About eleven others where we celebrated with

A huge stuffed turkey with
Cranberry jelly, raspberry jelly;
Potatoes; celery and hot bread;
Corn sauce; peas and salads.
For dessert, we had pumpkin pie

And fresh fruit salad.
We had no alcohol
Just grape lemonade
In chilled glasses,
With rims dipped in lemon and sugar.

The meal was finished off
With a good cup of hot coffee.
The evening ended with songs and a dance
And many memories to look back upon
In following years.

1980

Introduction to the Election

Comparing an English election with a Canadian election, I guess that things are pretty much the same in many respects. The fever and ferment of the last few days in Canada's local elections are something to experience.

There was an air of great excitement over the last few days before the final election of the Mayor, who would run the city of Calgary for a couple of years or so, to the best of his ability.

I quite enjoyed being a part of the elections in Calgary whilst I was there, although of course, being a mere visitor, I could not vote, so just watched!

Part I
Election Fever
Location: Calgary

I chose the month of October for my visit
Not only to see the
Changing climatic effects of the land,
But to take part in Thanksgiving Celebrations
And to experience Election Fever

Which had overtaken Calgary by storm.
There were banners and posters everywhere,
Television programmes promoting
Various men for the job.
In fact, for about two weeks

Before Election Day,
Competition was fierce,
Between a few men;
Then it was narrowed to three,
And each man presented himself

On television for a talk
About their policies.
On Election Night
A party of us went to a show
At the auditorium

Which is a lavish, modern place,
Just right for such extensive performances.
We went to hear Canadian massed choirs.
Before the show, everyone was
Talking about the election

And who would win.
Many of us had our favourites,
Including me, who was only a visitor.
As we settled in our seats
A hush descended,

The show commenced
And we listened in awe,
To the beautiful songs
Taken from Canada's history
Of long ago.

Midway in the evening,
A special announcement was made –
The man we had all hoped for,
Had won the Calgary Election,
And was looking forward to presenting his views

To Calgarians at some future date –
Everyone was overjoyed
At the results,
Stamping, and cheering
Resounded throughout the hall.

The show at the auditorium
Continued in full swing
And finished with
Canada's National Anthem,
Which always brings tears to my eyes.

We left the building en bloc
Jostling with members of the audience
All intent upon arriving at the car park
In one piece,
Climbing into the back and front seats

Of our car, we waited until the engine
Had warmed up, and the frost vanished
From the back and front windscreens,
Making vision for driving clearer
Along the frost laden roads;

Some distance out of Calgary,
We stopped at a farmhouse
For the promised cup of coffee
And delicious cake,
To catch up with gossip long overdue,

Returning to the ranch
At one in the morning,
When all the fields and hedgerows
Were heavily laden with frost,
And drooping under the weight.

1981-1982
Introduction to the Aftermath

Inflation has played a large part in the aftermath of the 1980 Election. The city is not the same as it was two years ago (as any English city suffering from the effects of inflation), even the people have changed, many of them being out of work, or afraid for the security of their jobs.

Calgary is the only city I have visited since the election of a new mayor – it is a shame that the city has had to suffer the effects of inflation before the mayor had a chance to finish off his plans.

I shall return to Calgary, if not this year, the following year, but I fear it will be a number of years before the city reverts back to its normal state of affairs.

Part II
The Aftermath
Location: Calgary

The years since the election
Have been good
To the Mayor Elect.

I heard from friends
That he has managed to achieve
Excellent results

For the city of Calgary –
A new light train service
From downtown Calgary to the south

Is one of the achievements,
And I believe, that they are considering
Extending the service northwards.

Other things have been achieved,
But I hear little news these days
Except for the occasional paper.

1982 has been a hard year
For inflation, and unemployment
Has arrived in Canada,

Taking its toll –
Collapsing businesses
As people run out of money

Has made the job of mayor
Doubly hard,
In fact, blame

Has probably been 'laid' at his door,
But it is not his fault,
For the world as a whole

Is suffering from inflationary effects,
Higher wages, and costs in the stores
Have brought about the closures

Of many businesses and companies,
With cutbacks in staff
Because of high costs and ground rates.

The unemployed just drift around
In the malls downtown,
Either doing nothing,

Or playing a guitar and singing
For a few dollars
To keep themselves alive.

Most of them look unkempt
For costs are too high to have hair
And whiskers trimmed.

Immigration from other countries
Has just been stopped,
For a Canadian has first offer

Of a job in his/her home country
Before an immigrant is considered,
Even if he or she has good qualifications.

However, there will come a day
When prosperity returns
As inflation decreases and normality resumes.

1981

Introduction to the Harvest Season

Alberta has everything to offer people from all 'walks of life'. If you are interested in farming or ranching and would like a working vacation, you can stay on a farm or ranch – it is surprising the number of interesting people I met from localised Canadian Ranches and overseas countries connected with farming.

I love to stay on a ranch, especially at harvest time, as it is such fun to help out, or maybe to just ride up and down on the truck with an old farm or ranch hand, listening to his tales of early Canadian ranching life.

I have met many ranchers and farmers on my visits to Alberta – they are all very interesting people and enjoy discussing their work, I learnt such a lot from them all.

Location of the Harvest Season at Balzac, Near the City of Calgary, Alberta

(Sketch Map, not to scale)

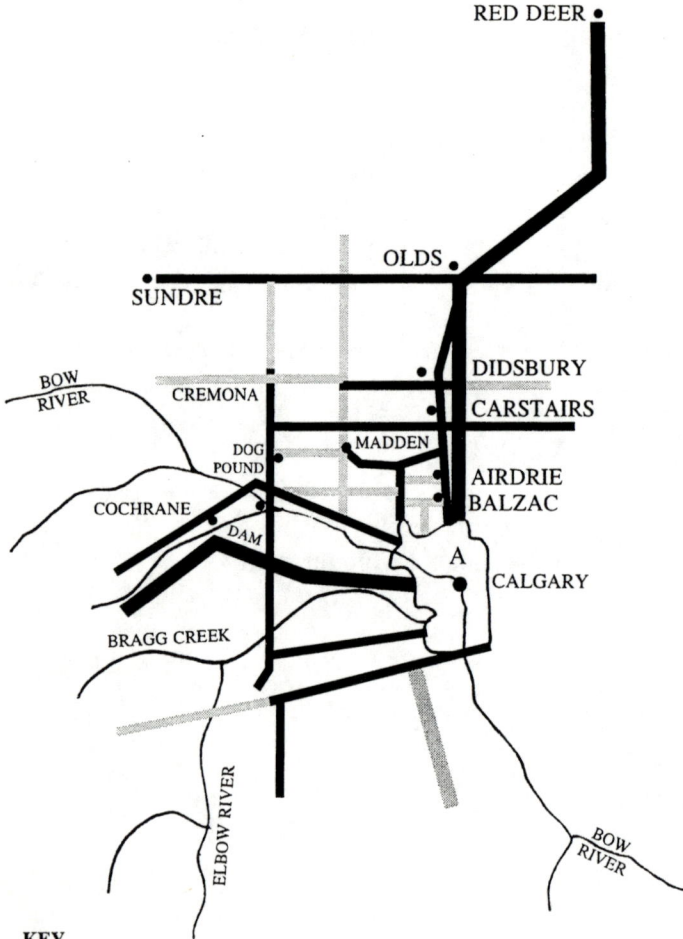

RED DEER

OLDS

SUNDRE

BOW RIVER

CREMONA

DIDSBURY

CARSTAIRS

DOG POUND

MADDEN

AIRDRIE

COCHRANE

DAM

BALZAC

A

CALGARY

BRAGG CREEK

ELBOW RIVER

BOW RIVER

KEY

PAVED ROADS

IMPROVED ROADS

4 LANES UNDIVIDED

DIVIDED HIGHWAY

AIRPORT   A

The Harvest Season
Part I
Harvesting

Depending upon the season,
September and October
Are usually harvest months
In Alberta.

The farmers and ranchers
Are often fortunate
With warm, dry weather, which is
Essential for keeping straw and grain dry.

An early start
Is the order of the day.
The owner of a ranch
Being the first astir during harvesting.

For, every moment counts,
Especially if the weather is variable.
As soon as the sun rises in the east,
The ranch is awake.

Sandwiches and coffee
Have been put aside
The night before,
Or, maybe,

The rancher's daughter,
And a friend,
Will walk over to the workers
At midday, with food and coffee.

Everyone, both workers and family, alike,
Gather around the table for
A huge breakfast
At five-thirty in the morning.

Both family, visitors,
And neighbouring ranchers
(Some from fifty miles away)
Rally around, and bring the harvest in.

One particular ranch
Used old-fashioned methods –
Not being able to afford
Expensive new machinery.

There were plenty of helpers
Willing to drive the tractors and trucks,
Up and down
And across the fields.

The tractor pulled the combine harvester,
Which separated the grain from the straw,
And stored it in the harvester
Till it was full,

At the same time, baling the straw
And dropping it off neatly at
The back of the combine harvester,
On to the ground.

Then, the truck,
Which had been following
The tractor,
Came alongside

Ready to take the grain
From the now, full combine harvester.
The grain was fed through a pipe
From the harvester to the truck.

When the truck was full,
It sped to the grain elevator
Or barn, and the tractor and
Harvester continued to work.

Part II
Threshing

In another area,
Two or three tractors
Were threshing,
And separating grain from chaff.

The hot sun shone mercilessly,
Out of a cloudless sky
Onto the heads of those below.
If heads were uncovered, or necks bared

This would result in sunstroke
Of a high degree.
Most people wore hats
Pulled low over the face,

Or, wore a scarf, maybe a bandanna
Around the neck,
For protection
Against the sun's rays.

A Blue Heeler, named Tornado,
Ran after the tractors,
Barking madly, and biting at the wheels,
Then, finally,

Jumping on to the back of a tractor,
Which his master drove,
Steadily up the field.
He sat panting, and watching

As they passed the old barn on the hill
Where the mice played,
In the winter months
Amidst the grain so deep.

At the top of the hill
The tractor turned,
Whilst the others
Went straight on,

Each turning at
An aforementioned point
To thresh the field,
Leaving no pile unthreshed.

Part III
Tornado's Adventures

Tornado saw a rabbit,
Which loitered
Near the haystack
Erected earlier that day.

Jumping off the back
Of the tractor,
He rushed off in strong pursuit.
The rabbit ran into the haystack.

Tornado ran after it
And succeeded in
Toppling the first half
Of the stack to the ground.

Amidst shouts of anguish
From his master,
He emerged from the
Pile of hay,

Shook himself and made off,
Down the hill
Without the rabbit,
Head down, and tail between legs,

He slunk out of sight,
Hoping to escape
His master's wrath, which he knew,
He would suffer from, that night.

The rabbit shot out of the stack,
Blundering into the tractor wheels'
He died,
Of fright, that very night!

So! Cooked rabbit
Would be on the menu
For dinner
The next night, after all.

Part IV
Rush Against Time

Meanwhile, the weather changed,
And it looked like rain.
A wind blew up,
It became quite cold.

The sky clouded over and the sun faded.
Eyes cast skywards,
Coats flung on, and in despair,
They desperately worked to save the crops.

For once wet, and flattened,
It would become difficult
To pick up, and,
Even harder to thresh.

This time,
They were lucky
And, the clouds passed over,
Leaving behind, a cooler atmosphere.

The wind blew and blew,
Setting the uncut corn waving
At the edges of the field.
Everyone breathed a sigh of relief.

We had escaped rain again!
But, somewhere else
It must have fallen,
And hard too, judging from the black sky

Moving slowly eastwards,
And out of sight
Around the back of the hill.
So, once again, the sun appeared

Bathing everything in a soft light,
Before sinking in a scarlet dome
On the western horizon,
Streaking the sky reddish yellow

Before vanishing from sight.
In an hour or two,
Dusk fell, and, in
Another five hours

They reckoned the job
Would be done
For yet another year.
But, first, a belated tea break.

Tools were laid aside
For fifteen minutes,
Whilst tea was drunk
And sandwiches of peanut butter consumed.

More help was forthcoming,
For they could see
Distant figures
Approaching in the dusk.

The daughter and son of the rancher
Wearing blue jeans and checked shirts
Came into sight,
Carrying cables and lighting,

Which they set up
Around the perimeter
Of the last field,
Waiting to be harvested,

In order to give
That added, extra light
To the workers,
So that no mistakes would be made

On this final vital field.
All four tractor drivers
Positioned their tractors
To start harvesting,

And the truck drivers
Climbed aboard their trucks,
Wiping dust and sweat
From their brows,

Leaving dirty streaks down their faces
In an attempt,
To keep the dirty sweat
From blinding them, as they drove along.

Part V
Dusk

The harvesting started again,
And the trucks followed the tractors,
Each positioning themselves
On a corner of the field.

The tractor headlamps came on,
And the trucks switched theirs on too,
So that all four corners of
The field were brightly illuminated,

Making it easier to see the
Harvest in progress.
The wind had dropped,
And a strong odour of skunk drifted in,

Destroying the sweet night perfumes.
Fortunately, the smell diminished,
As exhaust from the trucks
Rose into the air.

A good shower of rain
Was really required
To renew
The pleasant scents of the night.

It was very dark.
The huge, bright harvest moon
Was slowly rising
Into the deep, dark sky

Throwing its light
On to the workers below,
Anxious to finish the harvesting
And enjoy a belated hot meal

Before returning to their homes,
Accepting the rancher's hospitality,
Or retiring to their campers
Parked in the yard beyond.

The field was half-finished,
And the trucks
Newly filled with grain,
Had just departed for the grain elevators.

There were spotlights
Trained on the barns and elevators
So that the men could see easily
And not spill the grain

By an ill-timed movement
Which could cost them money
And give the mice a good meal,
To last them the winter through.

The tractors chugged along
And the harvesters
Separated the grain from the
Straw as fast as possible.

Part VI
The Final Acre

Tornado, the Blue Heeler,
Sat beside his master
On the leading tractor,
His keen eyes everywhere,

Looking for mischief
Or fun,
His master was grateful
For Tornado's company,

As harvesting was a lonely job.
He patted the dog on the head,
Who licked his hand
As he drove on.

His face was black
With dust and dirt,
But white, where the
Brim of his hat lay, over his brow.

He shifted in his seat,
Longing for the day's work
To be done.
Glancing round,

He saw
There were four more
Strips to be harvested,
And, then, they were finished.

He sighed,
"Thank goodness!
We are nearly done
For another year."

At long last
It was finished,
And the trucks
Made a final run to the barns.

The men,
Shutting off engines and headlights
Climbed stiffly down
From their tractors,

And, let their sons and daughters
Hovering in the background,
Take over,
Moving the tractors and trucks to the
    big barn

At the bottom of the hill,
Past the old binder
Which had stood there,
Derelict for years,

Having been left
As useless
By a rancher,
Several score years and ten ago.

They turned out the lights,
Disconnected the cables,
And flung plastic sheets
Over all, in case of a shower.

Yawning, and idly walking,
They set off together,
For the ranch
Nestling in the valley below.

1981

Introduction to a Fine Fall Day

The inspiration to write these few verses came from my viewing of the countryside on the day that I went for this lovely long walk.

Some of the verses are not true, but the verses relating to the nature of the land are quite true as it actually happened whilst I walked along, in fact, I could almost 'feel' the fanning of the whirring wings of the partridges against my face as I wrote those verses.

A Fine Fall Day

Location: Five miles north of Calgary, near Balzac

It was late afternoon,
And skies a bright unpolluted blue,
With sun shining brightly,
We set off for our walk
Across the harvested fields.

I carried a gun
In the hopes of spotting a rabbit
Or two for my dog's dinner.
It really was a beautiful day,
And, my heart felt light,

Bursting with happiness,
Not only because of the beautiful day,
For I was to be married
The following week,
To the boy of my dreams.

I came to the gate at the end of the field
A barbed wire stranded gate
With two posts at either end
And a loop from one post to the other,
Always difficult to unfasten, even if there
were two.

Jonah, my dog, jumped up,
Wanting to play.
I brushed him away
'Go! Play on your own!
I want to be alone!'

Walking alongside the wired fence
Deep in thought,
I saw nothing
Until it was too late.
A covey of partridge,

With young, were disturbed,
And flew up directly in front of my face
From the ground
Where they had their nest.
The whirring of their wings

And the speed which they flew up
From the ground
Scared me
As I thought
'My end' had come.

Jonah chased after them,
Hoping to catch his dinner
For the next night.
Unfortunately, he was not fast enough,
But enjoyed the exercise.

I wished then,
That I had brought
Along my camera
To record
The wonderful scene of nature.

Native Indian Bands, Reserves and Treaty Areas

(Sketch Map, not to scale)

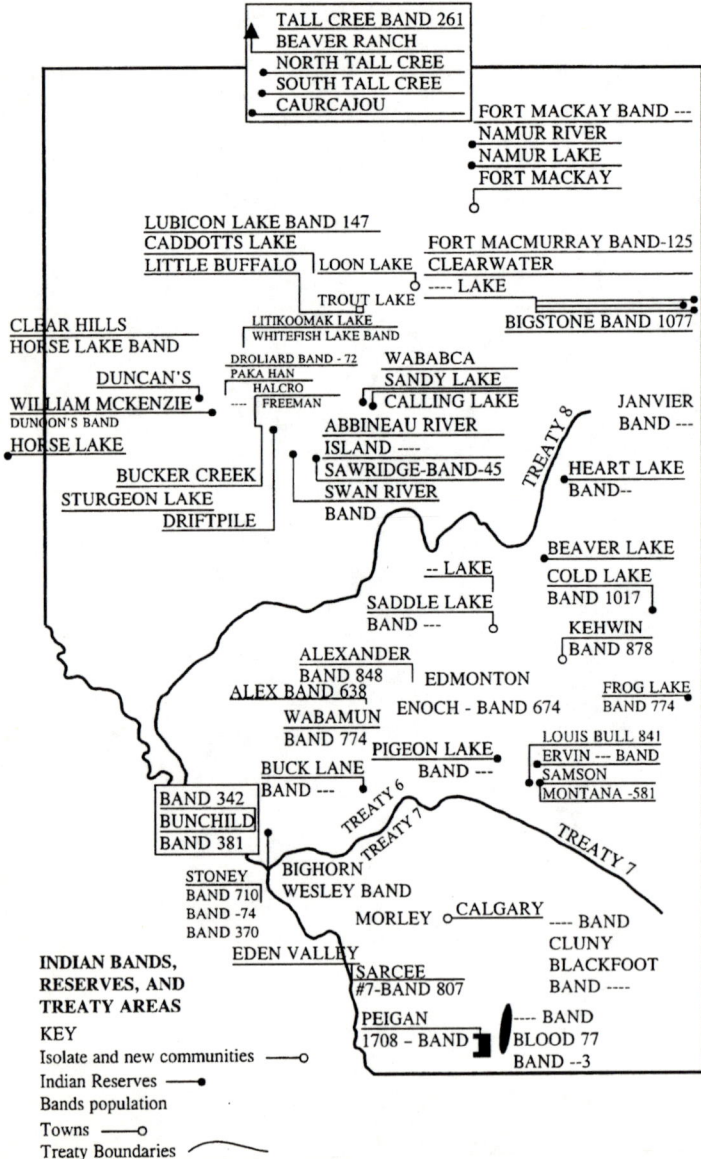

TALL CREE BAND 261
BEAVER RANCH
NORTH TALL CREE
SOUTH TALL CREE
CAURCAJOU

FORT MACKAY BAND ---
NAMUR RIVER
NAMUR LAKE
FORT MACKAY

LUBICON LAKE BAND 147
CADDOTTS LAKE
LITTLE BUFFALO
LOON LAKE
TROUT LAKE

FORT MACMURRAY BAND-125
CLEARWATER
---- LAKE

LITIKOOMAK LAKE
WHITEFISH LAKE BAND

BIGSTONE BAND 1077

CLEAR HILLS
HORSE LAKE BAND

DUNCAN'S
WILLIAM MCKENZIE
DUNCON'S BAND
HORSE LAKE

DROLIARD BAND - 72
PAKA HAN
HALCRO
FREEMAN

WABABCA
SANDY LAKE
CALLING LAKE

JANVIER
BAND ---

ABBINEAU RIVER
ISLAND ----
SAWRIDGE-BAND-45
SWAN RIVER
BAND

BUCKER CREEK
STURGEON LAKE
DRIFTPILE

TREATY 8

HEART LAKE
BAND--

-- LAKE
SADDLE LAKE
BAND ---

BEAVER LAKE
COLD LAKE
BAND 1017
KEHWIN
BAND 878

ALEXANDER
BAND 848
ALEX BAND 638
WABAMUN
BAND 774
BUCK LANE
BAND ---

EDMONTON

ENOCH - BAND 674

PIGEON LAKE
BAND ---

FROG LAKE
BAND 774

LOUIS BULL 841
ERVIN --- BAND
SAMSON
MONTANA -581

BAND 342
BUNCHILD
BAND 381

TREATY 6
TREATY 7

STONEY
BAND 710
BAND -74
BAND 370

BIGHORN
WESLEY BAND
MORLEY

TREATY 7

CALGARY

EDEN VALLEY

SARCEE
#7-BAND 807

PEIGAN
1708 – BAND

---- BAND
CLUNY
BLACKFOOT
BAND ----

---- BAND
BLOOD 77
BAND --3

**INDIAN BANDS,
RESERVES, AND
TREATY AREAS**

KEY
Isolate and new communities ——o
Indian Reserves ——●
Bands population
Towns ——o
Treaty Boundaries

1972–1983
Introduction to the Indian Nations of Alberta

I have always been fascinated by the Indian people of Alberta (and other provinces as well), even though the majority of 'White Men' seem to dislike the Indians for a variety of reasons.

I consider them to be extremely clever – many of them can foretell the future, they know what you are thinking of before you have even thought of it; in the past, as in the present, the Indian people can live on the land and survive from the 'fruits' of the land; they know the kinds of berries to collect for food; making tepees from buffalo hides, dying skins; smoking and tanning skins for clothing; making beadwork necklaces for the Indian handicraft stores on Reservations (and bartering with the tourists); making head dresses at The Calgary Stampede and Exhibition, Indian Village and hundreds of other things.

The following is an extract from a letter I received from the Culture Director (Chief) Harley Crowchild in 1983.

> In Alberta there are 42 American Indian Nations which consist of 3 Treaty areas – Treaty #6, Treaty #7, Treaty #8. [The map given to me by Harley Crowchild – TSÚ T'ÍNA K'OSA Sarcee Cultural Educational Programme – in 1983, which can be seen on the next page, will assist the reader to understand the locations.]
> Treaty #7 is made up of the Blackfoot, Bloods, Peigan, Sarcee (Tsú t'ína) and Stoney in the south. The language spoken by the Bloods, and Peigan is Algonquin; the Stoney Nation speaks the Sioux language

and the Sarcee (Tsú't'ína) speaks the Athapaskan language. The North American forefathers of the Indian Nations spoke 11 different languages and had a number of different ways of living – for example, the Plainsmen of North America were year round tourists, and the tepee living was their homes (very different from the other Indian homes of today's house trailers and tent trailers).

In 1877, Treaty #7 was signed in Southern Alberta, by Bloods, Peigan, Sarcee and Stoney Indians. In 1977, one hundred years later, the Treaty was re-enacted when Prince Charles visited Calgary.

Today, the Indian people either live in large cities or on their own reservations, but not in tepees any more as these are just museum or show pieces.

Indian Days are held every year in Alberta for members of the public to view the celebrations of Indian Nations participating in singing, games, making new friends and meeting old friends.

I have not yet had the opportunity to participate in the Alberta Indian Days, but I look forward to that time when it comes.

The Blood Indians are part of the great Blackfoot Nation which ruled the prairies of Alberta until 1880. Before the 'Old West' finally died, James Gladstone, known as 'Many Guns' or 'Akay-na-muka', a Blackfoot, was born in 1887 in Mountain Hill, Alberta. He went to an Anglican Mission School and at 18 became Chief Scout and Interpreter for the Royal Canadian North West Mounted Police and was based at Fort Macleod. He married the daughter of an important Blood Chief; was President of the Indian Association of Alberta for nine years and finally became the first Canadian native to be appointed to the Canadian Senate and served on the Committee for Indian affairs and this enabled treaty Indians to become eligible to vote in the 1962 Federal Elections. He died in 1971 of a heart attack. A mountain in Southern Alberta is named after James Gladstone as a tribute to him – a man who set an example to all Canadians.

Stoney Indian Nation

Despite considerable research I have only managed to write a little upon the Albertan Indians, but feel that the following information about the Stoney Indian Nation should be included as it is of historical importance and will assist readers in their understanding of Treaty #7 thus promoting good relationships between the 'Red Indians' and the 'White Peoples' about the history and culture of the Stoney Indians of Alberta.

Parts of the following script have been taken from the Stoney Indian Peoples Welcome to Visitors Report.

There are "three Bands within the Stoney Nation, each have their own Chief and Councillors – in 1983, the population was approximately 1,800 people."

> In the past, the Wesley Band lived in the 'headwaters' of the Red Deer and North Saskatchewan rivers, the Bearspaw Band lived in the Alberta foothills between Morley and Waterton Park, and the Chiniquay Band lived in the area along the Bow River.
> Together with the American Indian Nations previously mentioned on other pages, the Stoney Chiefs signed Treaty #7 in 1877 (re-enacted in 1977) which was an agreement between the Indian Nations and the Government of Canada. The signing of this Treaty meant that the Indian Nations could avoid similar wars with the Canadian Government to those which the United States of America experienced. If the Indian Nations had not agreed to this and other treaties there would have been wars in Canada and many 'white people' killed before the settlement of the 'Old West' took place.
> The Stoney Indians and other Indian Nations trusted the government officials and missionaries who came to speak with them and the treaties were signed in good faith.

Stoney Indians acted as guides for white people who came into the area and their forefathers assisted surveyors and construction crews to build the Trans Canada railroad which became such an important feature in Canada's development as a nation.

Historically, the Stoney Indians and other Indian Nations played an important part in the development of Canada.

Eventually, the Stoney Indian Nation intend to develop a museum within the grounds of their Reserve which will tell visitors more about the history, culture and development of the Stoney People.

Visitors are encouraged to this beautiful Reserve where the Indians love nature and the things the 'Great White Spirit' has created are kept as "close to nature as possible". Commercialisation would destroy the natural beauty of the area. The Stoney Indians would like everyone to visit them and share the wonders of creation by the 'Great White Spirit'.

A 'tepee village' has been built to help visitors understand how the 'Old West' Indians lived – Stoney Indian Nation's forefathers. Handicraft souvenirs can be bought at the local store, and are special as they are still used in Indian festivals, dances and ceremonial occasions and provide an income for the Stoney People.

Nearby is the old archaeological site (1800) of Old Bow Fort constructed by the fur traders and burned down by 'Red Indians' and abandoned.

Within the Reserve there is a Buffalo Paddock where the 'historical' animals can be seen. These animals played an vital part to the Plains Indian culture as they provided food, clothing, shelter, tools, and equipment to them and to the Stoney Nation forefathers. The destruction of the buffalo herds (see The Buffalo Jump Provincial Park story) brought changes to their cultural environment. Buffalo are dangerous, unpredictable animals and it is suggested that visitors do not approach them. Visitors who wish to take the trail to the mountains or wish to go fishing, can do so, providing special arrangements are made beforehand.

Other attractions are planned for the future development of the Reserve in future years.
For further information, (as at 1983), please contact:

The Stoney Indian Park Development, P.O. Box 10, Morley, Alberta, Canada.

I conclude with a wonderful poem which sums up everything I feel for the Indian Nations of Alberta.

For Her People

by Jeffrey H Canen

May the mountain's own Great Spirit
Make your life a singing stream;
May the twelve new moons now coming
Bring a purpose to your dreams.
May a rainbow touch your shoulder
With a promise in its glow;
May the sunlight fall upon you
As you walk in many snows.

The Historical Native Indian of Alberta
'Our Forefather'

Alberta Indian Days

Part I

Alberta Indians

Today, in the twentieth century,
The Indians
Live peaceably in reservations
On Alberta's land, and to name but a few –

Blackfoot, Blood, Peigan are found
In Southern Alberta.
The Sarcee Reservation is located
On the south-west boundary of Calgary city,

The Stoney Reservation is approximately
Twenty miles from Banff, north-west of Calgary;
Alberta's Indians are famed
For their horsemanship;

Their arts, crafts and highly decorated tepees
Are a great tourist attraction,
Both for visitors overseas
And the local Canadian inhabitants.

The Indian Ceremonial Dress
Is very colourful,
And draws great crowds
On Alberta Indian Days,

Or, at Calgary's Stampede.
Years ago,
And also, twentieth century,
Treaties were signed

(The latest Treaty signature being 1977)
Allowing Indians to have their own land
And money from the government of the day,
Providing they lived on the reservations

Instead of moving into local townships.
If they wanted to, the
Indian People became cultured
And started to live in wooden cabins,

Learning to read and write;
Attending their own schools,
Finally, finishing off at university
And having a career of their choice.

At first, it was very hard for the
Indian People to live inside a house or cabin
Like the 'White Man',[8]
As their life was under the stars –

The Indian People lived
As they were accustomed to,
Finding it hard to survive in a house,
And the Indian People became discouraged

---

[8] 'White Man' means no colour to the skin.

Turning to the land
To live as their forefathers had –
In skin tepees,[9] supported by saplings,
With a hole in the top for the smoke from fires;

Burying their dead on tiers
Constructed of saplings,
Leaving the bodies there till they rotted
With all personal possessions.

The burial ground was,
And still is,
Very special to the Indian Nations
Especially as they believe

The burial grounds are haunted
By the Great Spirits
Of their dead relations,
Or friends –

Then the second generation was born –
More skilled and educated they grew.
Schools, churches and homes were built,
And a reservation or two

---

[9] Original tepees were made of smoke tanned Buffalo hide (white hides were used in Summer for special occasions) supported by saplings of dry willow, poplar or jackpine. In winter snow was banked up around the tepees to keep out cold draughts.

Had Open Indian Days for the
'White Man' to see how clever the
Indian People had become.
In the past,

The Indian People were clever too,
For they had to survive
The cold of the land in winter,
And the drought of the summer.

Skins were turned into coats
After smoking and tanning;
Traps were laid to catch meat,
Berries were collected for dyes,

Frames were made for beadwork,
And there are many other useful
Handicrafts which the Indian People
Can make to draw money from the public.

Unfortunately, during the passage
Of the years, both the Indians and
'White Man' turned against each other.
Some 'White Men' deliberately

Gave the Indian People 'firewater' – whisky –
Which went to their heads
Far worse than the 'White Man';
For the Indians went completely wild,

And did not know what they were doing,
Shooting, and fighting in the streets,
Beating their womenfolk,
And, even taking the 'White Woman' off

To their tepees.
The 'White Man' disliked the
Clever way the Indians had
Of bartering for what they

Considered as poor workmanship, and other things,
Even today, the dislike is still there
In some unexplained way.
I know several people who feel like that.

It is interesting to be allowed on to
A reservation to see
The way the Indian People used to live –
They still have their tepees

All laid out in that special way,
The chief's being highly decorated,
And made of white skin,
The cooking utensils, the beadframes

And head dresses, traps and canoes
On display
Certainly give you some sort of idea
Of the way the Indian People used to live
    so many years ago.

It almost brings back memories
Of the final fight
Between 'White Man' and 'Red Man'
With six shooter, rifle, bow and arrow.

I was glad that I had visited a reservation
For I found it most interesting
To see what I had read about,
And was fascinated to watch

The making of a head dress
In feathers of many colours,
And, bows and arrows
With feathers and flint arrowheads.

1981

Introduction to Two Renegade 'Red Indians'

This incident really was quite amusing, of course, it was not at the time, for I really thought that I was going to become a squaw and would never see my home country again!

There is never usually anyone around at the times of distressful moments who could lend a helping hand!

In fact, when I ran into these two renegade 'Red Indians', the whole street was deserted!

It was a pity that someone had not been using a movie camera at that time, the results could have been quite interesting for a comedy movie.

Part II
Two Renegade[10] 'Red Indians'[11]
Location: downtown Calgary

One fine September day
My mother and I
Took the bus
Right downtown to Calgary.

We intended to tour the museum;
Calgary Tower; Indoor Gardens,
And shopping in
The mall, which is for pedestrians only.

Alighting from the bus
At Centre Street North,
We started to make our way
To the Calgary Tower in 9th Avenue.

The street was deserted
As all the buses and traffic
Turned south-east
Before 9th Avenue.

---

[10] 'Renegade' means separated from main band or tribe of Indians.
[11] Sunburnt colour of skin.

330

I was gazing into a shop window
When I felt a movement at my elbows.
Disregarding this, I stared on,
Lost in thought.

A sudden tug brought me down to earth
And instant horror!
Two renegade 'Red Indians'
Were trying to abduct me!

Their English was unintelligible.
They were tall, with long faces,
Black, straight hair
And a leather thong band around their heads.

Their chests were bare and brown
And they wore white buckskin fringed trousers,
With nothing on their feet.
They stood at least four inches above me

In height and were muscular,
But not too overweight,
And the pressure of their
Hands on my arms

Was strong,
Insistent that I should walk with them.
Against two of them
I had no chance

And, was momentarily frightened.
I pulled forward to get away,
Then tried to scream, but it
Ended in a squeak of fright,

For my mouth had dried up.
No one about, and no Mounties
To be seen
Who would be willing

To help a damsel in distress?
A flash back in my memory
Swam before the eyes –
Of days long ago

When Renegade 'Red Indians'
Plundered wagon trains and carried
Off the women to their tepees
To make them wives –

Oh no! I did not want to be a squaw!
I wanted to be free to see the world.
Finally, I managed to get away,
Pulling myself free.

My mother was unaware of my plight.
One minute I was there,
Then I had disappeared from sight,
Gone off with two strange men

Whom she felt sure were my friends!
I hastened to tell her
They were no one I knew, as yet,
But they surely had their eyes on me

For a wife!
We certainly had a tale to tell at the
End of our day,
About the Two Renegade 'Red Indians'.

1982

Introduction to Foothills Rodeo

I really loved my day at the Foothills Rodeo despite the rough weather.

I have the happy memories to look back upon for many a year, although I guess some folk prefer to forget them, especially if they fell from their horses, bulls or cows into all the slimy mud – quite amusing it was to see one of my friend's colleagues do just that! The fact that I filmed him with my movie camera did nothing to boost his ego either!

All that vast countryside and miles of nothing, but rolling hills and lakes with a background of trees of the Forestry Reserve, the very helpful members of the ranch, all helping to make the day one to remember.

Oh yes, I would dearly love to experience this day all over again some time.

Foothills Rodeo

Location: north-west of Cochrane

Part I
The Journey and Arrival

The company where my friends worked
Had their annual outing
On Saturday 26th June.

It was a lovely hot day
And the skies were blue.
We went to the sports stadium

To park the car
And step on chartered school buses,
Which was a novelty to me

As I had often seen the buses
On the streets of Calgary.
Everyone, both child and adult alike,

Were dressed in blue jeans and checked shirts,
Fully prepared with rainwear
For the expected thundershower during the day.

We boarded the waiting buses
One by one, and as they became full,
Set off from the car park and onto the road.

335

It took an hour-and-a-half to reach
Our destination, which was north-west
Of Cochrane, located in beautiful countryside.

The hills were towering high and rolling
On either side of the road,
And the higher we climbed,

The steeper and narrower the roads became
With sheer drops on either side,
And trickling streams or raging torrents of water.

We drove up a stony cattle gridded drive
With tall trees growing thickly on either side
For we were in the Foothills Forestry reserve area.

The drive was long,
And we passed several road forks
Before we finally reached the end of the trail.

It started to rain heavily
Before we reached our destination
And, by the time the buses parked in the fields

The rain was sheeting down.
We donned our waterproofs, and
The drivers shooed us out of the buses into the wet.

Crowds of people covered the
Green slopes of the hills,
Squelching their way to

Open topped canvas covered marquees.
I found half a dollar
And my friends found thirty cents.

It rained harder than ever –
As we say at home
'Like stair rods' –

We all reached comparative dryness
Just in time,
But even so

The canvas bulged in places, and
Where it sloped,
Water gathered in great pools

Which had to be brushed off
Before it leaked on to us
Through the seams,

And, beware,
If someone was standing
Near the entrance

When the deluge of water
Was dispersed,
For you were sure to get a bath!

We stood in little knots
All around the outskirts of the marquee
For the centre was open

In preparation for the huge fire
To be kindled when the
Square Dancing commenced later in the day.

The storm lasted an hour
And thunder, when it came, was loud,
Re-echoing all around.

The lightning was fierce and sheeted
Becoming very bright during the darkness of the
    storm,
The violence of it all quite frightened me.

During this period,
I was introduced to many colleagues and friends,
Then the sun came out and everything started
    steaming.

Part II
The Rodeo

We left the marquees,
Making our way
To the rodeo stands

Which were built on scaffolding
With wooden planks for seating.
We sat at the back, which was the highest
    point

For viewing,
Where there was an excellent view
Of ranch lands and the beautiful lake.

There were miles of nothing
Except for trees and the
Occasional cattle strung out, grazing,

Or, maybe, a horse rider or two,
Working with the cattle,
Possibly, just riding for pleasure.

We folded our jackets to sit on
As everything was dripping wet,
Damp, and cold to the body.

I was quite surprised
When I saw the lines of people
Waiting to be served beer –

Personally, I could never quite
Get used to the taste –
There were fizzy drinks for the children

And ice cream too.
The performance did not start
Until all beer drinkers had been served.

The rodeo enclosure
Was slimy with black muddy earth,
Pity the folk who would fall on to and into this!

A movie-maker was filming the crowds
And their expressions.
At one end of the enclosure

Was the commentator's stand
And the chute
Where the animals came in.

We had a good view
Of all the events
Which started with the Parade of Flags

And then, the Cowboys' Prayer,
Followed by competitors
On the Bucking Broncs;

Steer and bull riding;
Roping calves, holding them down
And roping steers too.

The bull riding
Could become quite dangerous
So, clowns were employed

To lead the bulls away
From the cowboys who fell off
Sooner than they expected.

There was a lot of fast talking
As the events took place,
I am quite sure the spokesman suffered
    a bad throat!

For the ladies,
There was fast barrel racing
Around three barrels

Placed far apart,
They were timed on their speed
And correctness of movement.

There was a 'free for all' event,
When members of the audience
Were persuaded to take part

In the roping and throwing
Of calves.
There was reluctance at first,

For the mud was truly churned up;
And I certainly would not have liked
To fall face downwards in all that muck!

We all had a good laugh
At the antics of colleagues and friends
Especially, when they 'bit the dust'!

Part III
The Barbecue

There was a mighty rush and a scramble
To get into lines
For the serving of hot food after the rodeo events.

The rump ends of calves were cooked on spits,
Over hot coals outside,
But there was plenty for everyone

With seconds for those who wished for more;
Hot rolls, accompanied with butter,
Were served, alongside with

A large jacket potato,
Soured cream and beans,
Including a side salad.

We each collected a tray for our food
And on the way to the marquees
Where benches and tables were laid out,

We picked up some apple pie,
And cold ginger ale,
With hot coffee to round off the meal.

There was a huge fire
Built of logs, in the middle
Of the marquee, on the grass,

Which is why a huge opening had
Been left in the top of the canvas,
For smoke to blow out.

We were surrounded by fir trees
And the mosquitoes
Had just started to come out,

But, with the heat of the fire,
It kept them at bay,
Hovering above us in small clouds.

Our meal was accompanied
By the strains of Square Dance music,
From a quintet of players

Who had been hired for the night
To keep us amused.
It was fun to watch the children dancing round

At their own pace.
We finished our meal,
And I sat back to talk to the colleagues of my
    friends,

About industrial life
Of a big oil company
In the twentieth century.

Part IV
The Square Dance

Before the square dancing commenced,
The rodeo prizes were awarded
With many a handclap.

The 'floor' for the dancing
Was just green grass,
Very muddy, after the tramp of feet.

In fact, during the evening,
The ground at one end of the 'floor'
Went up like a hill.

So, some clever person
Manufactured a wooden cross,
And placed it on the hump,

Saying it was 'Boot Hill'
Where all the good cowboys go!
It caused a laugh, enjoyed by all.

The quintet playing square dance music
Consisted of a fiddler, banjo player,
Guitarist and an accordionist,

As well as a caller.
I loved the sets they arranged,
And it was so funny to see people

Trying to learn new steps
In time with the music,
And getting into such a mess.

Everyone was laughing and enjoying it all.
I came to grief a few times
As the ground was uneven,

And when the pace was fast and furious,
I never looked at my feet,
The rhythm of the music swiftly moved me
    along.

Oh, I thoroughly enjoyed that night
Dancing around the piled log fire,
Talking to different people

And, generally, enjoying the atmosphere!
At dusk, lanterns were strung round
The open canvassed tent, and lit.

So, with the glow of the fire too,
It was indeed a romantic sight.
The skies were fading from a blue

To a velvet black, and the stars
Glittered far above in the heavens.
The perfume of nearby fir trees

After the heavy afternoon rains,
Wafted to me
At the slightest invitation of a breeze.

Part V
Homeward-Bound

The final ticket was bought
For that last drink
Which was hurriedly downed;

And, all too soon, it was time to go,
But, the buses could not leave
Until they had been well-filled

Otherwise, some people would
Be left behind
To spend the night on the ground!

Our bus was half-filled by quarter past eleven,
And we left
To travel the hazardous journey

Across rough countryside,
Which had no city lights
To guide us on our way.

The skies had clouded over
And the brilliant moon
Of a few hours ago, had vanished

Into the dark night.
Distant rumbles of thunder
Could be heard

And lightning flashes viewed,
But, we safely traversed
The perimeter of the ranch,

And came to the narrow roads
With the huge gorges on either side.
We held our breath at each corner we took,

As the headlights picked up
The deep drops
On either side of the road.

Although, some of us were so drunk
I do not think the passing scenery
Made much difference to them!

The nearer we came to the main highways
Leading us to Calgary,
Thunder and lightning,

Including heavy rain,
Increased in violence
Over the land.

By the time we reached the stadium
Where the cars were parked
It was pouring with rain.

Small puddles were huge lakes
Which covered the whole of the parking lot.
We alighted from the bus

And rushed over to the car,
Finding it impossible
To avoid wading through sheets of water.

Soon, we were safely back in the apartment
In south-west Calgary,
Enjoying a 'night cap'

And, remembering
The highlights
Of a really eventful day!

1982

Introduction to Airdrie Rodeo

I had not planned to go to this rodeo, and in fact, did not really know that it was taking place.

The rancher of the place where I was staying usually liked to go to most locally held rodeos, and he decided that he would 'up and go' to this rodeo, but as usual, I was the last to hear of his decision!

He just stood up after lunch, and looked at me wanting to know if I was coming – not wanting to miss out on anything, I collected my camera equipment and climbed into the car.

Off we went, soon catching up with miles of cars waiting to turn off into the temporary car park, where local officials smoothed the way for trouble free car parking.

The skies were overcast at first, but it soon warmed up when the sun came out.

I was introduced to an 'old timer', a school friend of the rancher I travelled with, and we passed a pleasant half hour or so chatting, until the rodeo began.

We sat on the hard ground, waiting for the show to begin. I felt an atmosphere of excitement all around me as we waited for the rodeo to start. The longer the beginning was delayed, the more impatient the crowds became.

After about an hour or so, the show commenced, much to the delight of everyone, the babbling ceased and all eyes riveted to the makeshift corral where events took place.

Not everyone likes to go to a rodeo show, but, for me, it is one of the delights of my life to see such fast moving, entertaining events.

Eventually, after the finals of all the shows in Alberta (I think I am right in saying this) the finalists take part in the greatest rodeo of all – The Calgary Stampede.

Location of Airdrie, Alberta, Exact Vicinity of Rodeo is not Indicated

(Sketch Map, not to scale)

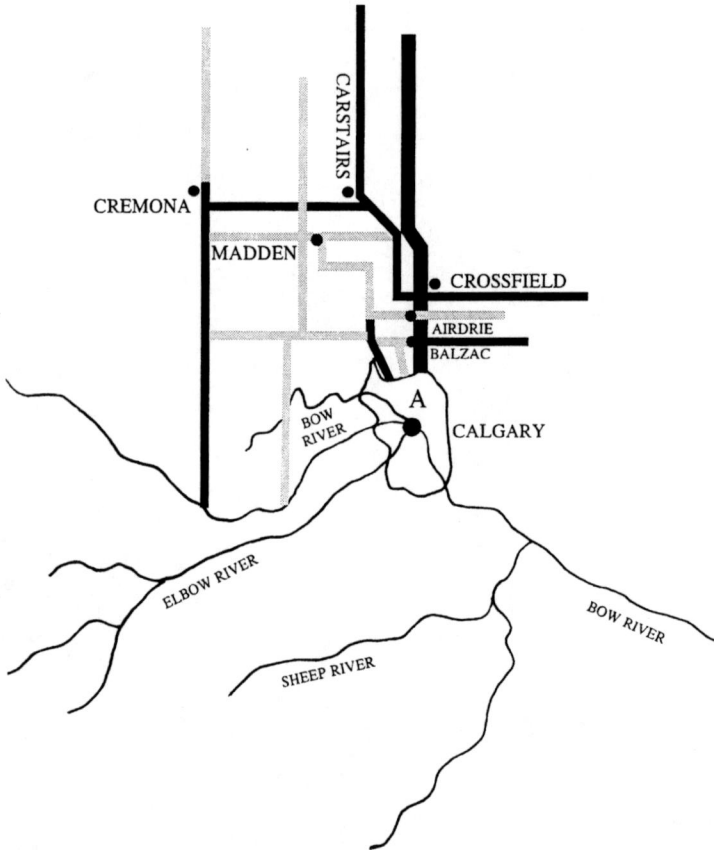

CARSTAIRS

CREMONA

MADDEN

CROSSFIELD

AIRDRIE

BALZAC

A

BOW RIVER

CALGARY

ELBOW RIVER

BOW RIVER

SHEEP RIVER

KEY

PAVED ROADS

IMPROVED ROADS

DIVIDED HIGHWAY

AIRPORT   A

Airdrie Rodeo

Location: a few miles north of Balzac

Part I

The Preparations

On a bit of waste ground
Just outside the town of Airdrie,
The Annual Rodeo is held –
Proceeds going to charity.

The rolling Alberta hills
Surround the rodeo grounds
Which are located at the bottom
Of an incline.

The rodeo grounds are enclosed
With corral-like fencing.
Canada and Alberta flags
Are flying at the top of the corral

Where the paramedics
Have their ambulance and first aiders,
And the television men have their cameras
And microphones to cover events.

Alongside the corral
Are the cattle pens
Where the bulls, cows,
And horses are penned

Prior to entering the chute
Which leads them to the
Rodeo grounds,
And competition with others.

Up on the hill
Food was in preparation.
The smell of cooked sausages
And hot popcorn

Wafted across the grounds
Making us feel very hungry,
Even though we had finished
Lunch over an hour ago.

A bit further round
And to the left
Stood a car with loudspeakers
Erected,

Playing distorted
Country and Western music
To keep the crowds happy
As they waited for the show to begin.

The delay,
Was because the television camera men
Could not get their microphones
To function, and had to send for new equipment.

I looked around and saw
Spectators of all shapes and sizes,
Sitting on coats, small chairs and stools,
All over the surrounding hill,

And as far as the eye could see,
No space of green
Was available
For anyone else to sit.

Behind my friend and I,
Tightly packed,
An untidy row of adults and
Children sprawled,

Their feet continually
Kicking against my back,
And the further I moved
Downhill, the more they moved.

Finally, I moved to
The other side
In order to get out of
Their way.

After a time,
The children and dogs
Became tired of
Waiting for the show to start,

And started to run wild
All over the hill,
Upsetting adults
And getting into mischief;

Ignoring the shouts
Of parents and dog owners,
Intent only,
On their games.

The grounds near the corral
Were very muddy and rutted,
With the occasional large puddle
Which small children liked to splash in.

The children just could not keep
Their fingers to themselves,
And started making mudpies,
Throwing them at each other;

Putting their fingers into the
Microphones left near the
Rodeo grounds
To record crowd sounds,

Loosening the nuts
So that the microphone
Fell off its perch,
Down on to the muddy ground.

There it stayed,
Until rescued
And removed
To a safer place.

The babble of voices
Grew very loud,
As 'old timers'
Met again;

And exchanged yarns,
Catching up with the gossip
Of a previous year.
New folk were getting acquainted;

Friends and relations
Were exchanging views
Or, maybe, making another date;
Lovers were arm-in-arm

As they made their way to the front,
Or rolled on the grass
Wet and damp as it was
Uncaring of future rheumatic pains!

Part II

The Action

It was a very hot day
The sun was in my eyes
And a hot wind blowing
Sunburned my face.

The sky looked stormy
In the east,
But, fortunately the storm
Passed us by.

In fact,
It encircled the grounds
All afternoon,
But no rains fell, nor thunder pealed.

The show started
When it was almost three in the afternoon.
Everyone stood up, silence falling,
For 'A Cowboy's Prayer';

Followed by the
Grand Entry Parade
And introduction of officials.
Finally 'Oh Canada' was sung
By a female soloist.

Afterwards, a great surge forwards
To view the events on the rodeo grounds.
Unthinkingly, the people standing
At the corral front blocked the view

Of those sitting on the slopes of the hill,
Making it impossible to see
Or take photographs of the exciting
Bareback Bronc Riding; Barrel Racing;

Calf Roping; Saddle Bronc Riding;
Steer Riding; Team Roping;
Wild Cow Milking;
Lastly, Bull Riding.

The first half of the rodeo
Before intermission,
Was fast and exciting
Including a few tumbles,

And sudden rushes by the paramedics
Anxious to help the injured
As they lay, groaning on the
Muddy and cold ground.

I liked the Bull Riding,
And the Wild Cow Milking
Best of all,
For there was never a dull moment.

Each time a cowboy fell off a bull
The rodeo clown
Would divert
The bull's attention

From the cowboy on the ground,
So that he would not
Be trodden on, or squashed.
There were a few very nasty moments

When a couple of them
Nearly came to grief,
But, for the quick thinking
Of the rodeo clown

The danger quickly passed,
And, the cowboys
Stood up
Trying to brush off caked mud

From their chaps
And brightly checked shirts,
As they made their way
Out of the rodeo grounds to safety.

My companion and I
Did not stay to the end of the show,
And the television men packed up
To go

In the early evening,
About six o'clock.
At this time, the air
Started to get chilly.

The sun went behind the clouds.
I pulled on my jacket,
Rising stiffly to my feet,
And started to walk up the hill,

Skirting sprawling people
Still intent
On watching the rodeo.
We walked past the desolate Midway,

Which had been busy
At intermission,
Giving rides to children,
And past blackened remains of the barbecue

Used to serve
Sausages and other refreshment,
Past the canvas tents
Where soft drinks were for sale,

And up to the
Flat plateau,
Where hundreds of cars
Were parked

In neat lines,
Side by side
On the green grass,
Quite long, in places.

There were some people
Having a picnic
Beside their cars,
And watching the rodeo too.

We were now feeling the cold,
And hurriedly
Entered the car
On our homeward trek.

Arriving back at the ranch
Half an hour later
We found visitors
Around the supper table

Looking forward to
Hearing all about
The 1982
Airdrie Rodeo Show.

1972–1982

Introduction to Memories

Memories are something you can continually look back upon, especially if they are illustrated with photographs and movie films, providing a source of pleasure for both family and friends.

In a sad moment of life, it is good to be able to look back upon the happy memories of the past – and in travelling to Alberta I have had many very happy memories, but unfortunately, there have been sad ones too, usually overcome by looking forward to the future with a happy smile.

I would never have come to Calgary if I had not had a penfriend there, to whom I had been writing since the age of eighteen.

I think it was one of the best moves I have ever made in my life, for now, I have done many things, including Western horse back riding (which is the pride of my life) into wilderness regions.

My mother, too, made an epic trip to Alberta in 1982, visiting as many of the places I could show her in our time allowance.

Memories

I was a stranger
When I arrived in Alberta
Ten years ago.

I came to the city of Calgary
Where I knew just one person
Who had been a penfriend to me

For several years
And now, I had a chance to meet
This friend, and see

The wonderful surroundings of that
Beautiful city,
I arrived at a tiny airport

With corrugated roof,
Just north of Calgary.
The airport was hot and airless

As there were no fans,
Small and cramped
With so many people around,

Packed tightly in long rows,
Awaiting to be cleared
Through Customs and Immigration.

The lines were long and
I became very tired,
But, still we waited,

Edging forwards
Inch by inch,
Pushing heavy luggage with our feet.

I had been lucky to find,
Before I arrived,
An accommodating ranch

In a travel brochure.
The people sounded very friendly
In their letters,

So I was reassured,
For to travel on my own
Was some great feat,

As at that time,
I was afraid of that
Great, Big, Old World.

I passed through the barriers
At last, and looked around
As I had no idea

What the folk looked like
I was going to meet.
There they were!

From descriptions
In their letters
I recognised them both,

One plump and the other
Tall and thin,
Welcoming and friendly,

As if I had known them both
For the whole of my life.
I had been apprehensive,

But not any more,
For all my fears
Had been washed away.

Off we went to the ranch
I had heard so much about
In the letters I received some months ago.

The countryside was beautiful
With vast rolling hills,
And the roads were straight,

With no bends, just valleys
And dips to please the eye,
And acres of crops,

Cattle and horses roaming the lands
Fenced in, of course,
For they all belong to the ranches

Dotted here and there,
Amidst the hills
So green, as it was early summer.

We reached the ranch at Balzac,
And I settled in with the other guests.
My first intention

Was to have a cabin
To hide myself away,
But they liked their guests

To mix with others
From all sorts of countries
And backgrounds,

Learning about each other,
Listening to their views,
And really,

It was the best thing
I ever did
To go to that ranch

And meet all those people,
Mingle with their family and friends,
Forget about myself and my fears

To become the real ME,
Gradually emerging from my shell
Over the ensuing years.

Many years have passed
Since that first travelling feat
And I have been back to that ranch

Hundreds of times,
But, of course,
Expansion has changed that land I love so
    much.

And things are not the same anymore.
The people are still there,
Older, but wiser.
I have lots of Albertan friends
Since I have taken time
Over the years

To travel from west to east,
And across most of the south
Over the province of Alberta.

I still have to visit
The northern regions,
But, I feel sure I will one day,

Adding more good, helpful friends
To my list
In Alberta

Where I now feel very much at home
And a stranger no more
Amongst the people I once regarded

As foreigners,
And now, they are some of my
Greatest friends.

These are only a few of my Albertan memories
Which have been portrayed in this book,
But there are many more to come.

Pen/Ink Drawing of Alberta Rose
(Rosa acicularis)

Colours usually varying from deep to light pink and white with yellow stamens and green leaves. The roses grow close to the ground and have very prickly stems. Some of them, as at Sylvan Lake, S Alberta, can grow several feet high.

The Alberta Flag

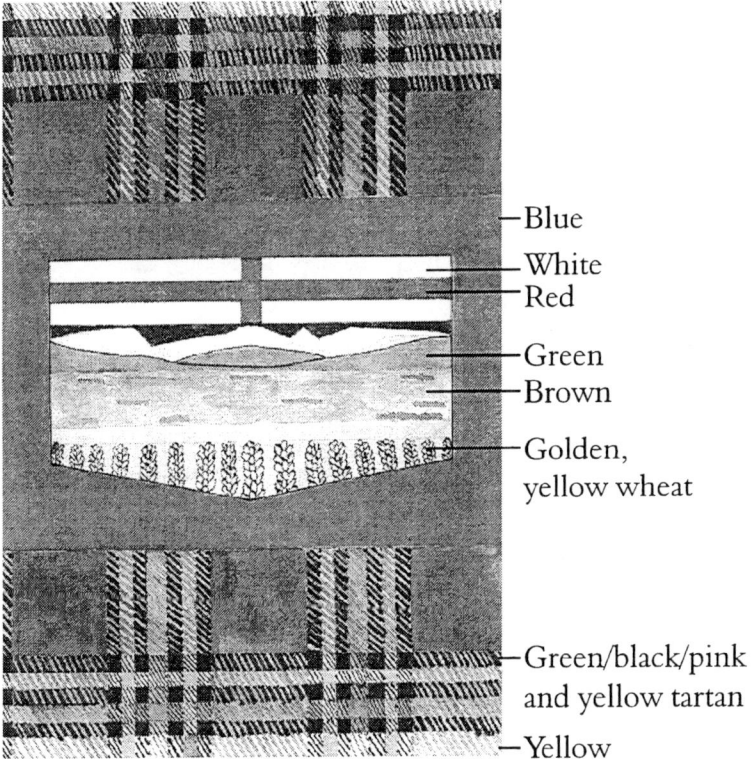

Blue
White
Red
Green
Brown
Golden, yellow wheat

Green/black/pink and yellow tartan
Yellow

(1)   Tartan: green for forests, black for mineral resources, coal/ petroleum, pink for wild rose, blue for clear skies and lakes.

(2)   Actual flag: red cross on white background, red for blood shed over the years, gold for fields of wheat, white for snow covered mountains/glaciers, brown and green for the rolling hills and prairies.

Epilogue

Little did I realize at the tender age of nine years in my Hampshire school days when I was photographed for the Anglo Canadian Trade Press of London NW3, that I would be travelling to Alberta, Canada in the 1970s-1980s – and writing a book!